THE COMIC STRIP CENTURY

THE COMIC STRIP CENTURY

Celebrating 100 Years of an American Art Form

Edited by Bill Blackbeard and Dale Crain

The Comic Strip Century. Published by O. G. Publishing Corp., 333 Sylvan Avenue, Suite 103, Englewood Cliffs, NJ 07628. Compilation © 1995 O. G. Publishing Corp. Introductory text © 1995 Bill Blackbeard. All rights reserved. No actual persons living or dead, are intended to be depicted nor should be inferred, but for instances of parody or satire. No reproduction is allowed without the consent of the publisher.

Distributed in the United States by Kitchen Sink Press, Inc., 320 Riverside Drive, Northampton, MA 01060.

Bill Blackbeard, Editor
Dale Crain, Co-Editor/Packager
James Vance, Associate Editor
Andreas Knigge, Consulting Editor
Rick Spanier, Typesetter
Rick Martin, black and white art restoration assistance

Library of Congress Cataloging-in-Publication Data
Comic strip century, 1896–1995 / edited and with an
   introduction by Bill Blackbeard.
      p.   cm.
   ISBN 0-87816-355-7
   1. Comic books, strips, etc.—United States.
   I. Blackbeard, Bill
PN6726.C66 1995
741.5'973—dc20   95-3574
                                   CIP

First printing: August 1995

9 8 7 6 5 4 3 2 1

All the comic strips were provided for reproduction by the San Francisco Academy of Comic Art. For further information write (enclosing a S.A.S.E.) to San Francisco Academy of Comic Art, 2850 Ulloa St., San Francisco, CA 94116.

Printed in Hong Kong.

Cover illustrations (left to right), details from:

Chic Young, *Blondie*, copyright © 1960 King Features Syndicate. Russell Keaton, *Flyin' Jenny*. Berke Breathed, *Bloom County*, copyright © 1988 The Washington Post Writers Group. Frank King, *Gasoline Alley*, copyright © 1921 Tribune Media Services. Roy Crane, *Wash Tubbs and Captain Easy*, copyright © 1933 United Media. Phil Nolan and Dick Calkins, *Buck Rogers*. George Herriman, *Krazy Kat*, copyright © 1937 King Features Syndicate. Al Capp, *Li'l Abner*, copyright © 1942 Capp Enterprises, Inc. Billy Debeck, *Barney Google*, copyright © 1929 King Features Syndicate. Harold Gray, *Little Orphan Annie*, copyright © 1933 Tribune Media Services. Hal Foster, *Prince Valiant*, copyright © 1950 King Features Syndicate. Ernie Bushmiller, *Nancy*, copyright © 1945 United Media. Winsor McCay, *Little Nemo in Slumberland*. George McManus, *Bringing Up Father*, copyright © 1953 King Features Syndicate. R. F. Outcault, *The Yellow Kid*. Walt Kelly, *Pogo*, copyright © 1957 Okeefenokee Glee and Perloo, Inc. Milton Caniff, *Terry and the Pirates*, copyright © 1935 Tribune Media Services. Chester Gould, *Dick Tracy*, copyright © 1944 Tribune Media Services. Alex Raymond, *Flash Gordon*, copyright © 1942 King Features Syndicate. Cliff Sterrett, *Polly and Her Pals*. V. T. Hamlin, *Alley Oop*, copyright © 1947 United Media. Otto Soglow, *The Little King*, copyright © 1935 King Features Syndicate. Lee Falk and Phil Davis, *Mandrake the Magician*, copyright © 1937 King Features Syndicate. Milt Gross, *Count Screwloose of Tooloose*. Charles Schulz, *Peanuts*, copyright © 1972 United Media. Sidney Smith, *The Gumps*, copyright © 1926 Tribune Media Services.

All comic strip work in this book first published after 1920 is in copyright. For specific and detailed copyright ownership listings see page 479.

Dedicated to...
   all of the comic strip artists and authors,
   all of the Newspaper strip syndicates,
   all of the Daily and Sunday newspapers,
   and all of the comic strip reprint publishers,
   past and present,
   who have made the magic and merriment of these pages
   possible through ten decades.
and to:
   the next century of comics already flowing vigorously from the
   pens of cartoonists and strip scripters around the world
   even as we read this remarkable record of the great work that
   has preceeded and inspired theirs.

                                —*Bill Blackbeard*

TABLE OF CONTENTS

VOLUME ONE

FOREWORD, *Dale Crain, James Vance* 7
INTRODUCTION, *Bill Blackbeard* 8
OVERVIEW, *Bill Blackbeard*
    PRECURSORS TO THE COMICS 10
    1900–1929 24
    1930–1939 28
    1940–1995 30

CHAPTER ONE: 1895–1919

HOGAN'S ALLEY (THE YELLOW KID), *R. F. Outcault* 35
THE KATZENJAMMER KIDS (HANS UND FRITZ, THE CAPTAIN
    AND THE KIDS), *Rudolph Dirks* 39
THE LITTLE BEARS, *James Swinnerton* 44
HUGO HERCULES, *J. Koerner* 45
MT. ARARAT, *James Swinnerton* 46
SUNDAY COMICS SECTION, HEARST NEWSPAPERS; 1904
    MT. ARARAT, *James Swinnerton* 47
    LULU AND LEANDER, *Frank M. Howarth* 48
    ALPHONSE AND GASTON, *Frederick Opper* 48
    HAPPY HOOLIGAN, *Frederick Opper* 49
    UNTITLED, *H. B. Martin* 49
    MT. ARARAT, *James Swinnerton* 50
    THE KATZENJAMMER KIDS, *Rudolph Dirks* 50
ALPHONSE AND GASTON, *Frederick Opper* 51
THE BROWNIES IN THE PHILIPPINES, *Palmer Cox* 57
ALPHONSE AND GASTON, *Frederick Opper* 58
ALPHONSE AND GASTON, THE KATZENJAMMER KIDS,
    AND HAPPY HOOLIGAN, *Frederick Opper*
    and *Rudolph Dirks* 60
HAPPY HOOLIGAN, *Frederick Opper* 62
MAUD, *Frederick Opper* 64
THE QUEER VISITORS FROM THE LAND OF OZ,
    L. Frank Baum and Walt McDougall 65
JIMMY, *James Swinnerton* 66
LITTLE SAMMY SNEEZE, *Winsor McCay* 66
HUNGRY HENRIETTA, *Winsor McCay* 67
DREAM OF THE RAREBIT FIEND, *Winsor McCay* 67
LITTLE NEMO IN SLUMBERLAND, *Winsor McCay* 68
BILLY BOUNCE, *Charles Kahles* 72
THE UPSIDE DOWNS, *Gustave Verbeck* 73
THE WOOZLEBEASTS, (*artist unknown*) 73
THE KIN-DER-KIDS, *Lyonel Feininger* 74
WEE WILLIE WINKIE'S WORLD, *Lyonel Feininger* 75
NIBSY THE NEWSBOY, *George McManus* 76
THE EXPLORIGATOR, *Harry Grant Dart* 77
MR. SKYGACK, FROM MARS, *A. D. Condo* 78
THE LITTLE JOURNEYS OF NIP AND TUCK, *John R. Neill* ... 79
THE FINEHEIMER TWINS, *Harold Knerr* 80
THE ADVENTURES OF MR. GEORGE, *Harold Knerr* 80
OLD OPIE DILLDOCK'S STORIES, *M. L. Wells* 81
SLIM JIM, *Raymond Crawford Ewer* 82
THE LITTLE POSSUM GANG, *C. M. Payne* 83
THE FAMILY UPSTAIRS, *George Herriman* 84

THE FIRST DAILY COMICS PAGE,
    HEARST NEWSPAPERS; JANUARY 31, 1912 91
    SILK HAT HARRY'S DIVORCE SUIT, *"Tad" Dorgan*
    THE DINGBAT FAMILY, *George Herriman*
    DESPERATE DESMOND, *Harry Hershfield*
    US BOYS, *Tom McNamara*
SHERLOCKO THE MONK, *Gus Mager* 92
OLD DOC YAK, *Sidney Smith* 93
MR. TWEE DEEDLE, *John Gruelle* 94
EVERETT TRUE, *A. D. Condo* 95
BUSTER BROWN, *R. F. Outcault* 96
PA'S IMPORTED SON-IN-LAW, *Ed Carey* 97
KRAZY KAT, *George Herriman* 98
BOBBY MAKE-BELIEVE, *Frank King* 106
BARON BEAN, *George Herriman* 107
MUTT AND JEFF, *Bud Fisher* 108
NOW LISTEN MABEL, *George Herriman* 110
MAMA'S ANGEL CHILD, *Penny Ross* 111
THE GUMPS, *Sidney Smith* 112

CHAPTER TWO: 1920–1929

BRINGING UP FATHER, *George McManus* 115
JERRY ON THE JOB, *Walter C. Hoban* 118
JUST BOY, *A. C. Fera* 120
STUMBLE INN, *George Herriman* 121
THE GUMPS, *Sidney Smith* 122
BARNEY GOOGLE, *Billy De Beck* 129
SUNDAY COMICS SECTION, HEARST NEWSPAPERS; 1924
    BRINGING UP FATHER, *George McManus* 147
    LITTLE JIMMY, *James Swinnerton* 148
    BARNEY GOOGLE, *Billy De Beck* 149
    TILLIE THE TOILER, *Russ Westover* 150
    BOOB McNUTT, *Rube Goldberg* 151
    HAPPY HOOLIGAN, *Frederick Opper* 152
    TOOTS AND CASPER, *Jimmy Murphy* 153
    THE KATZENJAMMER KIDS, *Harold Knerr* 154
POLLY AND HER PALS, *Cliff Sterrett* 155
HAIRBREADTH HARRY, *C. W. Kahles* 165
SALESMAN SAM, *George Swan* 167
THE KATZENJAMMER KIDS, *Harold Knerr* 168
TOONERVILLE FOLKS, *Fontaine Fox* 172
GASOLINE ALLEY, *Frank King* 174
WINNIE WINKLE, *Martin Branner* 177
THRILLING ADVENTURES OF COUNT BRIC A BRAC,
    Ludwig Bemelmans 179
SOMEBODY'S STENOG, *A. E. Hayward* 180
SKIPPY, *Percy Crosby* 182
NIZE BABY, *Milt Gross* 183
THE NEBBS, *Sol Hess* 184
MOON MULLINS, *Fred Willard* 185
THIMBLE THEATRE, *E. C. Segar* 200
EMBARRASSING MOMENTS, *George Herriman* 205
SCHOOL DAYS, *Clare Victor Dwiggins* 206
COUNT SCREWLOOSE OF TOOLOOSE, *Milt Gross* 209
DAVE'S DELICATESSEN, *Milt Gross* 210

CHAPTER THREE: 1930–1939

BOOB McNUTT, *Rube Goldberg* 213
FELIX, *Pat Sullivan* 216
THIMBLE THEATRE, *E. C. Segar* 217
JOE PALOOKA, *Ham Fisher* 222
BUCK ROGERS, *Phil Nowlan and Dick Calkins* ... 226
MICKEY MOUSE, *Walt Disney* 228
TAILSPIN TOMMY, *Glenn Chaffin and Hal Forrest* ... 232
CITY SHADOWS, *Percy Crosby* 233
JUST KIDS, *Ad Carter* 235
TIM TYLER'S LUCK, *Lyman Young* 236
DAN DUNN, *Norman Marsh* 237
BRONC PEELER, *Fred Harman* 240

VOLUME TWO

TERRY AND THE PIRATES, *Milton Caniff* 245
BLONDIE, *Chic Young* 250
THE LITTLE KING, *Otto Soglow* 274
SECRET AGENT X-9, *Dashiell Hammett and Alex Raymond* ... 275
THE ADVENTURES OF PATSY, *Mel Graff* 278
OUT OUR WAY, *J. R. Williams* 278
OUR BOARDING HOUSE, *Gene Ahern* 279
SCORCHY SMITH, *Noel Sickles* 279
THE KEWPIES, *Rose O'Neill* 282
DONNIE, *Darrell McClure* 283
HEJJI, *Dr. Seuss* 284
LITTLE JOE, *Ed Leffingwell* 296
SMILIN' JACK, *Zack Mosley* 297
HENRY, *Carl Anderson* 299
RED BARRY, *Will Gould* 300
THE BUNGLE FAMILY, *Harry J. Tuthill* 315
MINUTE MOVIES, *Ed Wheelan* 330
ALLEY OOP, *V. T. Hamlin* 344
LI'L ABNER, *Al Capp* 348
TINY TIM, *Stanley Link* 354
TARZAN, *Hal Foster, Burne Hogarth* 355
FLASH GORDON, JUNGLE JIM, *Alex Raymond* ... 362
LITTLE ORPHAN ANNIE, *Harold Gray* 366
DICK TRACY, *Chester Gould* 375
BRICK BRADFORD, *William Ritt and Clarence Gray* ... 379
THE SQUIRREL CAGE, *Gene Ahern* 380
THE PHANTOM, *Lee Falk and Ray Moore* 381
BARNEY BAXTER, *Frank Miller* 382
JIM HARDY, *Dick Moores* 382
RED RYDER, *Fred Harman* 383
MING FOO, *Brandon Walsh* 384
SMOKEY STOVER, *Bill Holman* 385
CONNIE, *Frank Godwin* 386
CAPTAIN EASY, *Roy Crane* 387
ABIE THE AGENT, *Harry Hershfield* 404
FRITZI RITZ, *Ernie Bushmiller* 406
NANCY, *Ernie Bushmiller* 407
MANDRAKE THE MAGICIAN, *Lee Falk and Phil Davis* ... 408
NAPOLEON, *Clifford McBride* 409
PRINCE VALIANT, *Hal Foster* 410

CHAPTER FOUR: 1940–1995

ABBIE AN' SLATS, *Raeburn Van Buren* 415
BRENDA STARR, *Dale Messick* 416
MYRA NORTH, *Ray Thompson and Charles Coll* ... 417
HUCKLEBERRY FINN, *Clare Victor Dwiggins* 417
THE RED KNIGHT, *John J. Welch and Jack W. McGuire* ... 418
BUNKY, *Billy De Beck* 419
THE PUSSYCAT PRINCESS, *Ed Anthony and Ruth Carroll* ... 422
SKIPPY, *Percy Crosby* 423
SUPERWOMAN, *Rea Irvin* 423
MISS FURY, *Tarpe Mills* 424
FLYIN' JENNY, *Frank Wead and Russell Keaton* ... 425
TEXAS SLIM, *Ferd Johnson* 426
BARNABY, *Crockett Johnson* 428
BATMAN AND ROBIN, *Bob Kane* 428
OAKY DOAKS, *R. B. Fuller* 429
SUPERMAN, *Jerry Siegel and Joe Shuster* 430
RIP KIRBY, *Alex Raymond* 431
BUZ SAWYER, *Roy Crane* 432
THE SPIRIT, *Will Eisner* 436
SILVER LININGS, *Harvey Kurtzman* 443
SAD SACK, *George Baker* 444
CASEY RUGGLES, *Warren Tufts* 445
STEVE CANYON, *Milton Caniff* 446
BEYOND MARS, *Jack Williamson and Lee Elias* ... 447
ARCHIE, *Bob Montana* 448
MIKE HAMMER, *Mickey Spillane and Ed Robbins* ... 450
BEETLE BAILEY, *Mort Walker* 451
POGO, *Walt Kelly* 455
RICK O'SHAY, *Stan Lynde* 459
ON STAGE, *Leonard Starr* 460
HI AND LOIS, *Mort Walker and Dik Browne* 460
SIR BAGBY, *R. and B. Hackney* 461
PEANUTS, *Charles Schulz* 462
DENNIS THE MENACE, *Hank Ketcham* 464
JOHNNY HAZARD, *Frank Robbins* 464
B.C., *Johnny Hart* 465
WIZARD OF ID, *Brant Parker and Johnny Hart* 465
GORDO, *Gus Arriola* 466
THE FAMILY CIRCUS, *Bil Keane* 467
BLOOM COUNTY, *Berke Breathed* 467
MOMMA, *Mell Lazarus* 467
ERNIE, *Bud Grace* 468
DOONESBURY, *G. B. Trudeau* 471
FOR BETTER OR WORSE, *Lynn Johnston* 472
FRANK AND ERNEST, *Bob Thaves* 472
ZIGGY, *Tom Wilson* 472
MOTHER GOOSE & GRIMM, *Mike Peters* 473
CATHY, *Cathy Guisewite* 473
ZIPPY THE PINHEAD, *Bill Griffith* 473
TUMBLEWEEDS, *T. K. Ryan* 473
SHOE, *Jeff MacNelly* 474
GARFIELD, *Jim Davis* 474
HAGAR, *Dik Browne* 474
CALVIN AND HOBBES, *Bill Watterson* 475
THE FAR SIDE, *Gary Larson* 476
GASOLINE ALLEY, *Jim Scancarelli* 476

INDEX 477
SELECTED BIBLIOGRAPHY 479

All titles appear in chronological order based upon the earliest date included; at that point all selections for each title are gathered in chronological order.

FOREWORD

HOW FIVE YEARS EQUALS A CENTURY
And, a 19th Century Distraction turns out to be not so Temporary

In 1990, with the one hundred year anniversary of the comic strip not all that far away, it occurred to me that a comprehensive historical collection of comic strips was not only due but almost required.

I had been involved in several collections of *individual* comic strip titles in their own books, many with David Li of Oceanic Graphic Printing, and the remarkable technological advances in color separation and printing I'd seen exemplified by David's work were the catalyst for this project. Never before has it been possible to reproduce vintage comics with the fidelity we are capable of today-full color sundays reproduced with all their brilliant and subtle rendering retained, the black and white dailies reprinted in richer black and on whiter paper than ever before.

As the packager, my first step was to solicit the services of Bill Blackbeard, the only qualified person who had the resources for a project like this; Quite simply, nobody knows more about comics, and as curator of the San Francisco Academy of Comic Art, he is the only person on earth who has literally at his fingertips copies of every nationally syndicated comic strip ever published. Bill came on board with an immediate enthusiasm, adding credibility and momentum to the project.

If there was a philosophy to our overall approach to the books contents, it was to provide as diverse a selection of comic strips as possible. Fortunately, in recent years many classic comic strips have been collected either in whole or in part and made available to the public. Therefore, those who might not agree with our choice to include only a handful of pages from *Terry and the Pirates*, for one example, are heartily encouraged to seek out the entire series of books reprinting the complete run of that strip.

Also, contemporary strips, which can be seen on a daily basis in newspapers or in their own book collections were given less exposure in favor of the older material which is virtually impossible to find outside of the few remaining newspaper morgues, a small number of university libraries and, of course the San Francisco Academy of Comic Art.

Bill Blackbeard compiled the initial list of strips to be included, European co-publisher Andreas Knigge, American distributor Denis Kitchen and I added our suggestions, and weeks were spent massaging the proposed list into a final form. At that point, Bill began forwarding the art for me to organize, and I began work on the overall structure of the book. It was necessary for me to add and (sometimes painfully) subtract from the selection of strips to be included up to, virtually, the very last minute of the five year process it required to transform my simple idea into massive reality.

All of which adds up to the largest high quality collection of the best examples of American comic strip art, ever. I can't imagine a better way to commemorate the one-hundred year anniversary of the comic strip.

In any project of this scope there are numerous people deserving of special thanks. Among those; David Li, whose support and hard work on this project made it possible; Bill Blackbeard, whose knowledge and resources were the foundation upon which this collection was built; Denis Kitchen, for his enthusiasm and commitment; Andreas Knigge, who was in at the beginning and somehow held on until the end, and because of that made this a better book; James Vance, for his sure editorial hand; Rick Spanier, the other half of "the machine," for technological support above and beyond duty; Rick Martin for his excellent work and deadline assistance; Chris Couch, Judith Hansen, and Scott Hyman of Kitchen Sink Press; Michael Lok, and the staff of O.G.P.; Art Spiegelman, inspiration and friend; and, especially to Jeanne Fong for her understanding, patience, and support.

—Dale Crain

Since its inception, the comic strip has always been seen as a disposable item—good for a few seconds' entertainment, preferably enjoyable enough to entice readers back to the next day's newspaper...but of no more deliberate importance or enduring value than the sports results, restaurant reviews or other examples of planned obsolescence that litter the history of modern journalism. Yet while reprint volumes of dining tips and boxing highlights are few and far between, there seems to be no end in sight to the number of books collecting comic strips.

It's a popular fallacy that old newspapers are heaps of flaking, yellowing pulp, but the condition of the strips reprinted in this volume, many of them in color as brilliant as the day they first saw print, should put the lie to that notion. It's only the original conception of them as disposable culture that's made them scarce, and only that scarcity which keeps most of us from enjoying them today.

This ambitious sampling of that colorful medium's first hundred years, featuring many strips never before collected in book form, should go a long way toward changing that undeserved status. Designed as a high-water mark among comic strip reference works, and featuring state-of-the-art reproduction from the lovingly preserved collection of Bill Blackbeard's San Francisco Academy of Comic Art, *The Comic Strip Century* is aimed at freeing the strips from archival obscurity and putting them back in the hands of their intended audience: the modern reader.

Whether the painstakingly rendered romantic fantasy of Harold Foster's *Tarzan* and *Prince Valiant*, the cunning political satire of Gary Trudeau's *Doonesbury*, or the rough-and-tumble smart-aleck romp of Will Gould's *Red Barry* (which seemed to dash headlong onto each day's page with pants unpressed and ink barely dry), comics at their best possess a peculiar charm and universal magic capable of reaching across the decades, continuing to speak to us not only of the lives of their fictional characters, but of the men and women who created and read them from day to day. They are, as Hamlet noted of another underappreciated medium, "the abstract and brief chronicles of the time"—and thanks to this volume, that time is with us still.

Let them be well used: enjoy this stroll through the first comic strip century...and be glad that some parts of our disposable culture are not so easily disposed of.

—James Vance

INTRODUCTION

THE DRAWN DRAMA
An Introductory Thought on the Art of the Comic Strip

When that leading American literary journal *The Bookman* gave serious and prolonged attention to the art of the newspaper comic strip in October and November, 1902, the magazine's staff made it quite clear that they were giving critical recognition to a *new* narrative art form (which they called "The New Humour"). *The Bookman's* editors, writers and readers were fully aware of the lively graphic pantomimes and text-captioned picture stories which had dominated graphic narrative style in the cartoon journals of the period, and they knew (having been in at its birth) that the newspaper strip was no minor adjustment of older graphic story forms, but a fresh and exciting innovation in narrative art.

Again, when Gilbert Seldes cited the newspaper comic strip as one of the lively new arts of his time in his seminal 1924 study *The Seven Lively Arts,* he didn't pontificate on its (non-existent) links to the classic picture story work of Gustave Doré and Wilhelm Busch from a hundred years before. Seldes treated it as a genuinely novel union of caricature and vaudeville, in which the strip form's utilization of the vital dialogue exchanges of the variety stage (in tight balloons near the drawn speakers' heads) had triggered the telling of fast-moving panel stories about verbally-realized graphic characters (making possible the compact narrative poetry of such works as *Krazy Kat* and *Little Nemo*), shorn of the pointless detritus of mechanical prose narrative repeating what was plainly going on in the story panels.[1]

H. T. Webster, 1924.

Not even Seldes or the *Bookman* staff, however — distracted as they understandably were by the firework display of four-color graphics in the Sunday strips — perceived the truly bizarre accomplishment of the new graphic story form. Few, in fact, then or now, would have been likely to note what would have seemed obvious to readers of the seventeenth and eighteenth centuries.

Steeped as everyone has been since the late 1700s in the ascendancy of prose fiction, the written drama (consisting of little beyond dialogue exchange) has become consigned to scholars on the one hand and to producers and directors on the other, to be enjoyed by the general public as "brought to life" on stage, television, or film. Yet it was the *convenience* of enjoying a complex story rapidly through dialogue alone that held back the development of narrative prose for so long. Shakespeare and Ben Johnson could have written superb novels if prose had been as popular a device for serious narrative and character development in their time as was performed and published drama. To the popular reader, however, such prose fiction as was then published was seen as *impeding* the natural character-to-character interplay that made reading drama such lively fun.

The new art of the comic strip, then, in effect restored the pleasures of reading dialogue drama to the general public, augmented by the new graphic portrayal of the actors themselves. While the magic of inspired prose narrative cannot be gainsaid, it remains perfectly true that the great characters of prose fiction have largely been realized through their dialogue, so that Pecksniff, Mrs. Gamp, Daisy Miller, Long John Silver and Leopold Bloom could move in graphic and spoken majesty from the pages of fiction to the comic strip format (in the hands of properly sympathetic and graphically gifted artists, of course) without any loss in their intrinsic impact as imaginative figures, even though divested of the rich prose garments which link them most directly to the pens of their creators.[2] Even more readily could the dialogue-evoked characters of Shakespeare, Jonson, Marlowe, Middleton, Sheridan and Wilde move to the comic strip page — *and* more usefully in terms of reader access than they have moved to film and television adaptation, since the author's dialogue would remain available on the page in conjunction with its visualization for ready rereading and reference.

Having thus somewhat augmented the prevailing perception of what the newspaper comic strip was and is (even in its sadly shrunken graphic stature in today's allotted space, with its current debilitating focus on kids and funny animals), we need only to move to the purpose of the present book, which is, simply, to illustrate the best and/or most typical work published from the newspaper strip's inception in 1896 to the present, as well as to seek out and illustrate the conceptual origins of the comic strip form in the decades prior to 1896. We will define and depict exactly what the comic strip is and is not, and trace its early erratic development from R. F. Outcault's remarkable *Yellow Kid* work to its fullest realization in the strips of Winsor McCay, George Herriman, E. C. Segar, Harold Gray, Chester Gould, Milt Gross and others over the past comic strip century.

This book does not pretend to be any kind of formal history of the comic strip in the hundreds of pages of detailed text such a work would of necessity entail, but it *is* meant to serve as a rich lode of select illustration for any subsequent history. So — go with Gross, Gould, and Gray, and enjoy!

— Bill Blackbeard

[1] Despite the essential silliness of this procedure, the prose-laden *Prince Valiant* comic page (which would have fitted perfectly into the cartoon story world of 1885) still continues successfully in many Sunday comic sections, while for years American comic book stories were absurdly freighted with unneeded explanatory prose which went quite sensibly ignored and unread by the majority of their ten-year-old audience. Happily, this meretricious mishandling of graphic narrative has been abandoned by the field in recent years, as has some of its single-minded catering to juveniles.

[2] We are speaking of ideal adaptations here, obviously. The less said about the criminal demeaning of famed fictional characters in the wretched art and bowdlerized rewriting of classic novels in the midcentury *Classic Comics* series of comic books, the better. They are best left to decay in the files of those who have invested in the phantom possibilities of long-term comic book values.

ONE | PRECURSORS OF THE COMICS

WHILE THE STAR WAS IN THE WINGS
How Nineteenth Century Literature Foreshadowed the Comic Strip

The Comic Strip Century was the only title ever considered for this book. Given the scope and content of the two volumes, it's a sound title and a sensible one. After all, we've had newspaper comic strips in the United States and a large part of the world during the whole of the twentieth century. A hundred-year wrapup is obviously a good idea. But…why in 1995?

Since the comic strip as we know it — a serial sequential narrative in drawn panels featuring recurrent characters in an open-ended series of stories, told by explanatory dialogue balloons *within* the story panels with little or no narrative text — didn't become widespread in newspapers until Fred Opper made regular weekly use of the new narrative art form in his hugely popular *Happy Hooligan* Sunday page from 1900 on, it would seem to make sense to hold off a hundred-year anthology until the actual end of the present century.

But — and this is the fascinating part — the new art form which Opper put to such happy use didn't itself exist *anywhere* in the world until October 25, 1896, when a young Sunday newspaper cartoonist already famous for a color panel series based on New York City slum kid life changed his regular format and, for the first time in the history of graphic art, drew an episode that incorporated balloon dialogue crucial to understanding the gag, thus also creating the first comic strip episode. The cartoonist's name was Richard Felton Outcault, his already-famed panel series was known as *Hogan's Alley,* and the innovative new format featured the central figure of the series, the immensely popular Yellow Kid.

The comic strip format then, not generally in continual use until after 1900, was nevertheless *born* in 1896, and any useful calculation of the scope of the comic strip era must begin with that date. 1995, accordingly, gives this set of survey volumes the opportunity to be in print throughout the actual anniversary year and serve as a reference well into the second comic strip century.

But why wasn't the offhand Outcault creation of 1896 not recognized at once as the incredibly innovative and universally useful gift to comic art narrative it was going to become after 1900? Why didn't Outcault himself realize what he had invented and make full use of it through the remaining years of *The Yellow Kid* (as *Hogan's Alley* later came to be called)? We'll look into the specifics of this question later — there is some evidence that Outcault *did* in fact understand what he was doing in the water- shed 1896 episode and in a few similar episodes he drew at the time — but in general, the blame can be put on simple conceptual drag: the understandable disinterest of the public and newspaper cartoonists of the time in going beyond the already wildly successful if essentially static format of captioned cartoon panels and sequences, to pay dubious attention to a crucially interdependent balloon text-and-picture concept that would have to be confronted and enjoyed in a whole new way.

Tentative moves in the direction of the comic strip format in the past, notably Marie Duval's brilliant sequences featuring her Ally Sloper creation for the English magazine *Judy* in the 1860s and '70s, failed to spark further development (the Duval stories were in fact replaced by large single captioned panels featuring Sloper, drawn by another artist in the 1880s and later). The weight of format tradition in cartoon art was simply not ready for a transformation in 1896; even four years later it took the determined efforts of the most widely respected comic artist of the time, Fred Opper, given free rein by publisher William Randolph Hearst, to make a real and lasting impact on the format of Sunday newspaper comics.

To pursue the chronological arrangement of *The Comic Strip Century,* and get a full perspective on the foreshadowings of the comic strip art form created by Outcault, it may be worthwhile to take a considerable step back from the 1890s for a fresh look at the old, well-chewed subject of the history of the comic strip.

And I *do* mean a fresh look.

For a hundred years before 1896, the fundamental concept of the newspaper comic strip was tremblingly close to being realized, with the functional equivalent of comic strips being hugely enjoyed by tens of thousands of suspense-gripped readers in England and America, waiting regularly at newsstands and bookstalls to continue following the work of the finest creators of fiction and cartoon art as it was periodically published in continued installments.

Clearly, in view of the above outlines of the comic strip's actual background, we are not going to pursue strip art origins in another artist-to-artist survey of static gag cartoon art in the nineteenth century, let alone in a pointless study of the caricature broadsides of the eighteenth. Broadsides were political and social commentaries, having virtually no connection with fictional narrative and character, while the gag cartoon, found in its classic mode in *Punch* from 1841 on, has long been a self-sufficient art field of its own, developing a parlous latter-day relationship with the comic strip only in such infrequent print-captioned, character-centered newspaper panel series as *Dennis the Menace, Mr. Tweedy,* and *Charlie.* (Parlous, since any such series could *become* a comic strip by the simple expedient of replacing its archaic printed captions with lively hand-lettered dialogue balloons — in fact, gag cartoons *per se*, from the *New Yorker* to *Playboy*, could be given greater artistic integrity and visual appeal by just such a sensible transformation.)

The attempt of some strip historians to find definitive comic strip work in certain captioned mid-nineteenth century magazine cartoon series featuring a continuing character (such as the slapstick hilarity of Marie Duval's Ally Sloper in *Judy* or John Leech's somewhat soberer John Thomas anecdotes in *Punch*) brings us fairly close to the real conceptual background of the comic strip, if not its actual execution; but the essentially anecdotal nature of these works, even though shorn at times of the heavy and unnecessary textual burden that usually accompanied them, coupled with their lack of any prolonged inter-episodic continuity, makes it clear that this is a false if seemingly promising trail. We are going to set this material aside and instead take a long and revealing look at the genuine, crucial conceptual origin of the comic strip narrative form from its outset in English book illustration early in the nineteenth century to its dwindling demise in the 1870s. Amazingly, that ignored, overlooked, unheralded origin, once perceived, seems the most obvious thing in the world: obvious even in its parallel development and decline to that of the American newspaper comic strip narrative form that succeeded it. So obvious that, like Poe's purloined letter, it has been altogether too visible to be noted as such.

Imagine the impossible. Conjure up a time and place in which cartoon art is the accepted *norm* in illustration, posters, and advertisements. All magazine covers and serial novel covers are the work of cartoonists. Cartoon art is accepted in oil and watercolor, and sells for top money in the best salons. Cartoon originals are prized on every level of society. Yet the word cartoon itself, as applied to this kind of art, is unknown to the broad public which revels in the cartooncopia that shapes the nature of popular and high art everywhere. Instead, the prevailing cartoon art is routinely called "illustrations," "book and magazine cover art," "poster art," etc., just as if such art were the natural way to develop such material and called for no special descriptive term of its own. Cartoons rule. It's a cartoon world.

A nice fantasy, you say? An engaging cloudland reverie? And so it would seem to be — until we realize that this impossibility actually existed at the turn of the nineteenth century in England and continued to hold sway for the next fifty years. Some of the most eminent figures of English literature were intimately involved with this apotheosis of cartoon art: Dickens, Thackeray (himself a gifted cartoonist), Trollope, Reade, Ainsworth, Marryat, and a myriad of lesser lights, all of whom regarded the best of their cartoonist illustrators and collaborators as men of equal eminence and talent to themselves.

Several of the best-selling novels of the period developed from characters made famous by the books' illustrators — such renowned cartoonists as Thomas Rowlandson, George Cruikshank and his father tried to recoup investments in poorly written fiction projects by spiffing them up with illustrations by one or another of the nation's top cartoonists, such as "Phiz" (Hablot Knight Browne, Dickens' illustrative collaborator) or Robert Seymour (whose art helped launch Dickens' career).

Rowlandson, Cruikshank, Phiz, Leech, Tenniel (the cartoonist who illustrated the *Alice* books), Seymour, and others were household names among the educated and the masses alike in the England of this enchanted half-century or so, and shelf after shelf of novels, poetry, children's books, books on war, books on naval exploits — you name it — in private homes were filled as much with prose as with cartoon art. *Punch,* the biggest magazine success of mid-century England, was jammed with little more than cartoon art, interspersed with pithy verse and commentary, and its imitators were legion.

Newsstands, crowded with the latest installments of thirty or more continuing novels-in-parts (the popular path of new fiction at the time), cheek by jowl with a bright-covered array of such author-edited journals as *Bentley's Miscellany, The Cornhill,* and *Ainworth's Magazine,* and edged with the continually-selling annuals and monthlies of such cartoonists as Cruikshank, Rowlandson, and Leech, turned bower-faces of cartoon fancy to a delighted public. Shops in every neighborhood hawked fresh lots of political caricatures and social comments by the nation's cartoonists in water-colored prints every week, while poster-bills for current dramas, comedies, vaudeville shows and revels run up on the blind sides of city buildings were wrought almost wholly in cartoon art. Water colors and occasional oils by Rowlandson, Cruikshank, Leech, Phiz, and others sold well in the London galleries and were hung in country houses across England. The sceptered isle was a sea of cartoon art in those years, and the public swam happily in it as if it would never end.

The word "cartoon" itself was used during most of this period only to refer to the preliminary sketches painters made before undertaking murals or easel oils. Light slang use of the term among artists for line drawings in general was taken up by writers at *Punch* in the early 1840s, and first appeared in print there as descriptive of a humorous drawing in an issue dated July 15, 1843. Popular use of the new term followed, but was limited for decades to come to gags or funny drawings only: illustrations to popular novels, for example, even though done by artists drawing "funny pictures" in *Punch* in the same style, were not termed cartoon art until much later in the century. What we now call cartoon art in general, no matter how it was employed (even in so scarifying a work as *Maus*), was seen in the 1800–1850 period and later as simply a richly enjoyable *style* of art, applicable, as such, to any and all artistic themes or subjects without any sense of its use in some areas as inappropriate. Seen in such a light, cartoon art takes on a much larger significance than the twentieth century in general has seen fit to give it.

As a style, applied in nineteenth century novel illustration to tragic, suspenseful, tender, and horrific subjects as well as comic, cartoon art emerges as an attractively easy, open technique, utilizing various degrees of exaggeration for the depiction of all subjects, usually to enlarge and focus the effect and to provide the artist range for the application of individual graphic techniques in both figures and backgrounds. This last was useful in giving an artist's work instant recognition. In modern magazine fiction illustration as seen in its best in the *Saturday Evening Post* and *Collier's* in the 1930s and 1940s, most of the illustrators were visually indistinguishable from each other to the layman without checking signatures or making a close study of technique; in contrast, the English artists of 1800–1850 could be identified at a glance by anyone in any work they did. Strict reality was eschewed

Cartoonist George Cruikshank's fine, fierce, deadly serious action illustration for M. H. Barker's *Tough Yarns* (1835).

by the English artists, logically enough, as imposing restraints on stylistic freedom and forcing painstaking attention to detail which in the last analysis is usually irrelevant to mood or point.

Never before and never again were artists and authors so closely and vitally linked in the co-creation of the highest levels of art and literature as during that halcyon English age. Famed artists depended on writers to illustrate *their* story and character concepts in appropriate text, as much as writers leaned on artists to bring their prose creations to vivid graphic life. Dickens, a touchstone through all of this period, began his career as a young author illustrated by the top cartoonist of the time (to ensure the book's sale), turned to writing fiction continuity to carry the cartoon creations of another noted artist through their paces, and entered the major phase of his career working in close harness with a third great cartoonist on nearly a dozen shared novels for over twenty years.

Dickens' involved relations with these three cartoonists are typical of those which prevailed between many artists and authors of the time, and will serve to epitomize the primary aspect of this colorful era which concerns us here: the production of long narrative fiction in tight tandem cooperation between writer and artist with heavy emphasis on recurrent characters developing as written and drawn against deadline for weekly or monthly newsstand publication, a common undertaking at the time which exactly anticipates and parallels the newspaper strip and comic book work of our time.

From the first decade of the nineteenth century it became increasingly popular for new novels (whether inspired by artist or author or both) to be published in weekly or monthly parts bound with advertisements into stiff illustrated covers and sold in bookstores, news stalls, and similar places. When the authors and artists saw fit to wind up their often picaresque, loosely plotted narratives, the collected parts were often bound by the purchasers into permanent book form, while the original publishers issued other bound sets for bookstore sale.

As reprinted later through the century, the original illustrations were almost always included with the text; it was only after it became the "vogue" to publish fiction without illustrations in the 1880s or so (abetted by publishers who wanted to avoid the expense) that the manifold editions of Victorian and Edwardian fiction lacking the original illustrations we see everywhere today became the rule. The damage done to the structure of many of these works by dropping the original illustrations which author and artist had so carefully worked together to incorporate as an integral part of the narrative has only recently been grasped by the critical world, notably in the cases of Dickens and Thackeray, and the art is returning to many new editions of these books.

When a famous artist of the period, Robert Seymour, noted for his skilled comic handling of Cockney sportsmen, proposed an idea for a serial novel dealing with a middle-class hunting club in London taking off on a picaresque tour of the provinces, the artist's publisher thought of a bright young writer named

Charles Dickens (who had just published a collection of humorous short stories called *Sketches by Boz* with illustrations by George Cruikshank) as a likely man to do the accompanying narrative text, with Dickens to take his story instructions from Seymour. The idea, normal for the time, worked out exactly in reverse. Dickens, ebullient and overflowing with comic ideas, overwhelmed the then-ailing Seymour with a three-chapter text for the first monthly number of *The Posthumous Papers of the Pickwick Club* (later simply *The Pickwick Papers*) that trampled his simple ideas underfoot in the soaring heights of fancy to which Dickens took them.

The publisher, like the public, was amazed at the new comic talent that had burst on the serial scene, and it was obvious to everyone but Seymour that Dickens had taken charge of the whole project. Now the artist had to draw to Dickens' demands, a situation so shocking to a man who had always been in charge of such undertakings before that he promptly died — partly of his illness, partly of simple dismay. Dickens was distressed at what had happened, seeing that he had been thoughtlessly careless in the cavalier way he had dealt with the famed cartoonist, and realized he would have to deal with his subsequent illustrator on *Pickwick* on a more evenhanded basis.

Happily, this proved to be no problem with the artist who signed aboard the novel by the time the fourth issue was due to be written. Hablot Knight Browne (who promptly dubbed himself "Phiz" to match Dickens' "Boz" byline on *Pickwick*) was a genial genius whose perceptions of character and drama meshed with those of Dickens from the first. So happily launched, their *Pickwick* rollicked on through another seventeen parts to become the widest-selling serial (and, later, book) of its time. The reputations of both artist and author were made; they were hot as a cracker, and only Dickens' obligation to a magazine publisher who serialized his next novel, *Oliver Twist*, and wanted Cruikshank as illustrator, caused him to part with Browne even briefly. With his following newsstand novel-in-parts, *Nicholas Nickleby*, Dickens rejoined Browne with gusto, and the two were not to part again until twenty years and another nine novels had rolled by.

On every level but the elimination of narrative text and the multiplication of Browne's cartoon panels to accommodate the flow of Dickens' dialogue, the activities and end results of the collaboration of these two matchless talents might as well have been stimulated by the production of a weekly newspaper comic strip or a monthly comic book. Detailed plotting and story outline by Dickens seldom extended more than one or two novel parts ahead, while Browne had to turn out his art in a fixed period of time each month as he received Dickens' precise suggestions for the illustrations. At the outset of a new novel, just as with a new comic strip, Dickens and Browne would huddle and work over graphic sketches of the principal characters slated to open the work, as well as over the elaborate cover design that identified the issues of each new novel on the newsstands.

Much of the fiction of this period resembled newspaper strip story lines of the 1920s and 1930s with its rapid narrative swing between the comic and the melodramatic. Dickens' bizarre character comedy and fanciful plots in his novels before 1850 are much like E. C. Segar's; Captain Marryat's brutal and exciting sea stories, populated with both comic and horrific adventures, closely resemble Roy Crane's work at its best; Thackeray's acid domestic exchanges and handling of social-climbing con-men parallel those in Harry J. Tuthill's *Bungle Family*, and the cartoon illustrations heighten the similarity. As one pages through the hundred and fifty-year-old bound volumes of these many novels-in-parts, it is as if time had stood still, so crisp and alive is much of the prose, so gripping the action, so undated the comedy, and it is easy to see the cartoon illustrations transferred to the Sunday comic pages of the 1920–1930 period, when strong story lines and comic characters developed in depth ruled the newspaper roost and the strip was at its brief apogee in the United States.

Martin Chuzzlewit and *The Old Curiosity Shop*, with their great cargoes of classic human caricatures, from Mrs. Gamp, Mr. Pecksniff, and Sally and Sampson Brass, to Chevy Slyme, Montague Tigg, and the vicious Quilp, can easily be imagined as running for years in the color strip pages (Dickens' novels are wondrously long, like strips) beside *Moon Mullins, Thimble Theatre*, and *Dick Tracy*, and cozily bylined "Boz and Phiz." The extant illustrations, too, can readily be imagined as fitting into the linking panels necessary for a full-fleshed comic strip, augmented with dialogue balloons richly laden (in the spatial opportunities of the pre-1940s comic page) with the comic and dramatic exchanges of Dickens' raucous characters.

In the first Phiz illustration reproduced here, we see a richly satiric scene portrayed from Dickens' *Martin Chuzzlewit*, in which the peripatetic Martin and his travelling companion from England, Mark Tapley, are confronted in the rowdy editorial offices of a slezoid newspaper office in New York by the publisher, one "Colonel" Diver, and his sixteen-year-old "war correspondent," Mr. Jefferson Brick. Following this raucous turn, the following cut finds Phiz sensitively catching the edgy, mean mood of a cache of scoundrels sounding out each other's motives and plots as their surface conversation maintains a largely polite tone. This is the "Mr. Nadgett" cut, again from *Martin Chuzzlewit*, portraying a London scene occurring during Martin's American excursion. Jonas Chuzzlewit, who will later murder the suave Montague Tigg who is applying the double brushes so dexterously to his sveltely barbered locks, has been momentarily crushed by some savage implications in Tigg's genial remarks, while the darkly listening party who stands apart in the background warming his scarf by the fire processes the gist of what he hears in terms of what he knows. Known only as Nadgett, he is the first private eye in English literature, and a scurvy, skulking figure he is — exactly as caught by Phiz. A passage in this chapter, describing Jonas' reaction a bit later to a really alarming charge by Tigg, again gives us a neat sense of Dickens' bright, cartoon prose…and way with horror.

"[Tigg] beckoned to Jonas to bring his chair nearer; and looking slightly round, as if to remind him of the presence of Nadgett, whispered in his ear.

"From red to white; from white to red again; from red to yellow; then to a cold, dull, awful, sweat-bedabbled blue. In the short whisper, all these changes fell upon the face of Jonas Chuzzlewit; and when at last he laid his hand upon the whisperer's mouth, appalled, lest any syllable of what he said should reach the ears of the third person present, it was as bloodless and as heavy as the hand of death."

In a grim scene from the London underworld, "Secret Intelligence," from *Dombey and Son*, Phiz demonstrates the brutal realism with which the cartoonist illustrators of the time would depict poverty. In this drawing there is not the least flinching from the grubby ugliness of life obviously lived in one room. Again, the dramatic tension of a Dickens scene is perfectly caught, with the shrill importunities of the bonneted harridan, the echoing gabble of the caged parrot, and the despair of the couple seated at

Illustration by Phiz from Dicken's *Pickwick Papers* (1836), showing the cartoon image of Pickwick that became wildly popular around the world.

Illustration by Phiz from Dicken's *Martin Chuzzlewit* (1843).

Martin Chuzzlewit illustration: Phiz (1843), showing the first private eye in English fiction, Mr. Nadgett.

Illustration by Phiz from Dicken's *Dombey and Son* (1847).

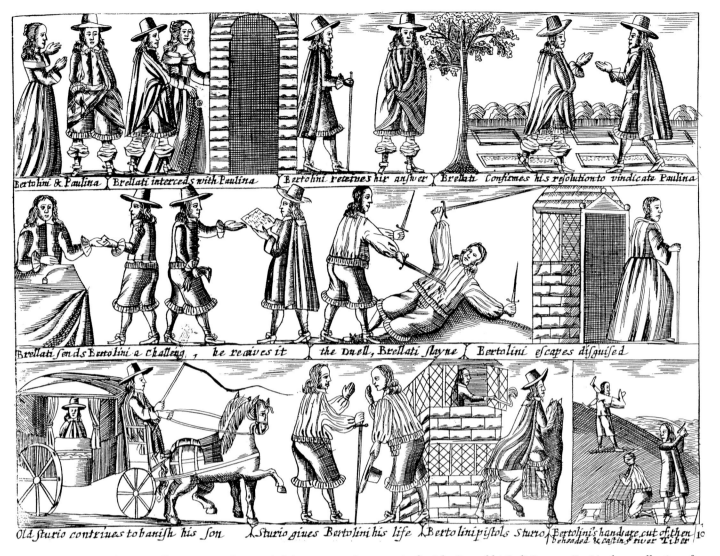

First sequential-panel cartoon illustration work in English literature; unknown artist for John Reynolds' *God's Revenge For Murder*, a collection of short crime fiction from 1656.

the table, unaware of the lowering presence of Mr. Dombey at the door. It is a scene Harold Gray could have caught perfectly as well in illustrating *Dombey,* just as Phiz could have depicted the story line of *Orphan Annie* without ever losing the mood or drama of Gray's actual art.

Dickens, Phiz, and Cruikshank have made the case. But we need to briefly document and summarize a few other high points in the origin and development of the nineteenth century illustrated novel in newsstand serial parts, if only to have an entertaining look at some of the other widely renowned cartoon characters of the period that emerged from this extraordinary fifty-year body of material.

Our golden age of cartoon illustration began in 1809, when a print and sometime book publisher named Rudolph Ackermann decided to combine the enormously popular satiric broadside print art of the greatest cartoonist of the day, Thomas Rowlandson, with selections of light humorous doggerel in a new periodical to be called the *Political Magazine.* As a novel attraction, Ackermann asked Rowlandson to lampoon the popular (and very serious) illustrated discourses on British scenery by one Samuel Ireland, whose endless series of "Picturesque" views of everything from the Isle of Wight to the Isle of Dogs had gotten to seem funny to Britons.

Rowlandson invented an angular, dryasdust schoolmaster in retirement named Doctor Syntax, who self-elected himself to make a scholarly tour of British beauty spots and to star in a monthly verse serial for the Ackermann magazine, to be called in its final book form *The Tour of Dr. Syntax in Search of the Picturesque.* Needless to say, Dr. Syntax's exploits led him into comic disasters, as superbly limned in the two color plates Rowlandson drew for each monthly part, and rather maladroitly narrated in the verse text written around the Rowlandson drawings by William Combe, a contemporary hack previously employed by Ackermann on other publications. (Ackermann kept Combe on a short leash: he was a regular inmate of Debtor's Prison at the time, and paid for his coffee and cakes out of an "expenses" stipend Ackermann maintained for him.)

Unexpectedly, the Dr. Syntax adventures and art became a vogue, and then a craze. Just as happened with the newspaper strips *Yellow Kid, Popeye* and *Peanuts* a century and more later, toy and gimmick manufacturers seized on the public delight with the blundering schoolmaster and reproduced his image in a thousand forms — as Toby mugs, puppets, tops, dinnerware design, figurines, an adopted figure in political cartoons, and as a star in at least a half dozen stage adaptations. Enlarged prints of the Rowlandson illustrations hung in country homes as commonly as in coffee houses and gin palaces. Even Combe's leaden verses

were quoted glibly to receptive applause at dinner parties across Britain. The first Syntax volume was followed by two more during the ensuing decade, and was imitated in popular works by other hands as Doctor Comicus and Doctor Prosody.

No sooner had the Syntax welcome finally worn thin than a sporting writer and editor named Pierce Egan, who in 1820 had begun to publish a fictionalized account of high and low life in London in monthly parts, contacted a pair of roisterous drinking buddies — who also happened to be the brother cartoonists Robert and George Cruikshank — and asked them illustrate the work. The result, based on their personal inspections of palaces and boozing kens across the nocturnal metropolis, and called *Life in London; or, the Day and Night Scenes of Jerry Hawthorne, Esq. and his elegant friend Corinthian Tom, accompanied by Bob Logic, the Oxonian, in their Rambles and Sprees through the Metropolis,* was an almost immediate hit with the young sophisticated crowd of the late Georgian era, and swiftly ballooned into a national craze to rival that of Doctor Syntax. Once again there were toys, statuettes, plateware, and prints on sale on every street, celebrating the Cruikshank drawings of notorious London scenes and the images of the three urban explorers, Tom, Jerry, and Bob (thin disguises for the author and artists, of course), and again there were stage adaptations and book-in-part imitations called *Life in Paris, Life in Ireland, Real Life in London,* and so on. Egan's text, aside from being prose, was the plodding equivalent of Combe's verse, and held readers primarily though its exciting timeliness and continuous use of underworld argot, which fascinated the public; as with Rowlandson's Syntax drawings, it was the Cruikshank cartoon work that really fostered the ongoing craze and etched the images of the book's heroes into the public fancy.

Two illustrations by Rowlandson from William Combe's *Dr. Syntax* series (1810): another immensely popular 19th century cartoon character portrayal.

A final book in 1830, Egan's *Finish to the Adventures of Tom, Jerry, and Logic in their Pursuits through Life in and out of London*, illustrated by Robert Cruikshank alone this time, wrapped up the hot vogue for the Egan world at just about the point that the raucous Georgian period gave way to the Victorian era.

Although Charles Dickens' *Sketches by Boz* was illustrated by George Cruikshank in the same gamey and roistering manner he had used to spice *Life in London*, it was not until Dickens' real genius for story and comic character emerged in *The Posthumous Papers of the Pickwick Club* in 1836, in company with the designs of a new young cartoonist named Hablot Knight Browne, that London was again seized with a cartoon character obsession that surpassed even those engendered by the ungainly Syntax or the outrageous Egan trio. Dickens' Mr. Pickwick and his fellow members of the Pickwick Club (briefly drawn at first by Robert Seymour and R. W. Buss) exploded into real graphic life at the pen of the imaginative Browne in the fourth monthly issue of the new novel in parts. But the real difference in the creation of this fresh English craze for a book and its cartoon characters from the two that had preceded it was that here the author, not the artist, was the true motivating genius behind both the narrative and the art. Dickens, who had grown up with Syntax and Egan, felt it was crucial to popular success in fiction to effectively combine story and cartoon art, and in consequence he worked closely with Browne on every one of the hundreds of drawings the cartoonist was to make for *Pickwick* and almost a dozen subsequent novels in parts.

The huge success of *Pickwick* led a number of publishers and authors in London to launch their own illustrated novels in parts, with such writers as W. Harrison Ainsworth, Charles Lever, Thackeray, Trollope, Harry Cockton, and many others publishing dozens of monthly-part novels over the next three decades, utilizing the cartoon talents of Robert and George Cruikshank, Browne (as "Phiz," of course; he did not limit his work to Dickens' novels), John Leech, Thomas Onwhyn, Richard Doyle, Samuel Lover (who, like Thackeray, wrote and illustrated his own novels), and a myriad of others, famed and unfamed, who confronted the British reading public with a world of popular literature, all appearing weekly or monthly, and all with each and every story unforgettably framed in a consistently high level of cartoon art.

Unfortunately for this long-lived high tide of comic art and great literature, the era that had made it possible was drawing to a close. For almost three quarters of the nineteenth century, the reading public read pretty much what it liked, with no guilt over "taste" or "literary art." True, a few writers here and there, such as Bulwer-Lytton, made noises about form and structure in fiction, echoed by some savagely destructive critics in early literary journals, but the public and writers in general paid them little heed.

A new generation of writers, however, which began to mature in the 1870s and later, determined — as all new crops of writers traditionally are — to ride roughshod over the work and attitudes of their predecessors, were greatly impressed by such fresh talents as George Meredith and Henry James, who frankly wrote for "art" and without much concern for entertainment values in fiction. Immediately championed by the critical and academic coteries (who had long and fruitlessly deplored murders and melodrama and suspense and high comedy in the highly popular fiction of Dickens, Wilkie Collins, Charles Reade, and even Bulwer-Lytton himself: indeed virtually all English fiction writers of the time), the new writers, and a new generation of publishers and editors, proceeded to turn the literary and illustration world of the immediate past upside down.

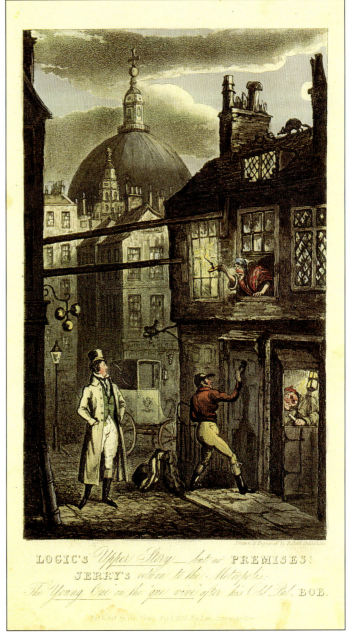

Illustration by Robert Cruikshank from Pierce Egan's *Tom and Jerry* series (1830).

All at once, cartoon art was old hat as fiction illustration, to be replaced by dense, grim, gray, hyper-realistic (and calculatedly static and dull) drawings by salon artists such as Millais and Burne-Jones, who in turn were aped by new illustrators such as Charles Keene, Fred Walker, Arthur Hughes, M. J. Lawless, and a sorry lot of similarly talented but wholly humorless young men, all of whose illustrations seemed to have been etched in deep charcoal, with darkness prevailing everywhere and the twitch of precise detail filling every possible open space. It is from the prevalence of such work in the later decades of the century — it even took over in *Punch* and other establishment humor magazines — that much of today's view of the Victorian era as a grim and bleak and artistically ugly time derives.

The cartoonists? They went where too many of them are still found — to children's books, to the story-papers for boys and girls, and to lowbrow gag cartoon magazines.

And, of course, to the newspaper comic strips. They had, indeed, been thrown out of paradise.

A pretty close parallel can be drawn between the rise and fall of the great cartoon-illustration age in England (when for the first time cartoonists developed story and character in depth over long periods of time for periodical publication, just as they were later to do in newspaper comics) and the rise and fall of the comic strip era in American newspapers. But we will be observing this latter matter at length throughout these two volumes, while at this point it should be useful to look at some of the most memorable cartoon work done in the nineteenth century by artists largely uninvolved with periodical novel-part illustration. Since these are primarily the cartoonists covered in a marvelously detailed and superbly illustrated study of the last century's gag cartoon in England, Europe, and America, and its curious occasional prose-and-panel thrusts toward comic strip structure, edited by David Kunzle and named (quite misleadingly) *The History of the Comic Strip: The Nineteenth Century,* there is no need to do more here than touch on a few of the artists who developed interesting if functionally remote comic strip antecedents.

The picture story — a series of pantomime or captioned panels sequentially outlining the progress of an event (usually slapstick) or a linked series of events, with or without identifiable characters, and almost never published in periodical episodes — is clearly an extended variant of the gag cartoon and political caricature, and in most cases is more of an antithesis of the comic strip than its virtual predecessor. Historically, it can be traced to such commemorative political works as the Bayeux Tapestry and the Column of Trajan in Rome, emerging in its earliest form most memorably in the highly realistic social caricature portfolios and paintings of William Hogarth in the early eighteenth century. Most later artists reduced the Hogarth concept of detailed individual prints of each panel to be stacked and read in order or mounted in sequence on walls, to much smaller cartoon panels linked in story sequence on a single print. Among the great political print caricaturists of the later eighteenth century who utilized this format (though infrequently) were James Gillray, Rowlandson, and Isaac Cruikshank, father of George and Robert.

This same format — the picture story *per se* — seems to have been used in social comment (i.e., slapstick gags based on daily life), but surviving broadside examples are much scarcer than the political works prior to the nineteenth century. The idea of extended stories printed apart from the broadside market and published as booklets did not noticeably find public sale until one Rudolphe Töppfer began to publish his work in 1835 to considerable acclaim. A Swiss school teacher and minor author, Töppfer had been encouraged by appreciations of a number of "picture novels" he had drawn to entertain his pupils in a rapid, loose cartoon style with narrative text beneath each panel. (One such encourager was none less than Goethe himself, who had been hand-carried some of the Töppfer cartoon MSS for his delectation.)

While Töppfer's tendency toward illogical and even irrational narrative development in some "novels" was criticized, the bulk of his work, with its simplistic but highly entertaining visual horseplay based on the antics of pedagogues, scientists, children and dogs, was much to the taste of the German reading public. His narrative format itself seems to have met with no public surprise, chiefly because such originally home-drawn picture narratives were then common in European households wherever a modicum of graphic talent existed with one family member or another. (In 1840, no less a personage than Alfred de Musset drew a brilliantly witty fifteen-page picture "novel" reflecting on his loss of one Pauline Garcia to a large-nosed rival named Louis Viardot; drawn strictly for private entertainment, it was finally published in 1964.) Many writers, from Thackeray to H. G. Wells, drew such picture stories as adolescents; found in their files decades later, some were eventually printed.

Far more accomplished in the picture story than the slapdash Töppfer (and we must bear in mind that this minor gag cartoon format was never seen as anything unusual or remarkable at the time; it was an occasionally useful device for a cartoonist, nothing more) was a French artist named Amadèè de Noè, who drew under the byline Cham. One of three inarguable geniuses who drew extensively in cartoon narrative in the nineteenth century (the other two were Wilhelm Busch and Marie Duval), Cham's most popular work in this line was a series of fictionalized comic accounts of his travels around Europe and abroad, but his major production was a long, witty, and incisive pictorial narrative commenting on the structural and social absurdities of Victor Hugo's monumental tirade against his own idea of social injustice in France, *Les Miserables.*

Published serially in *Le Journal Amusant* over many weeks in 1862 and '63, Cham's counter-epic was called simply *Les Miserables de Victor Hugo.* To anyone readily put off by the imaginative excesses of Hugo's titanic and largely humorless fulmination against social tyranny, Cham's gentle, devastating satire is as much of a delight now as it must have been at the time. Dealing as it does with recurrent characters and appearing weekly, Cham's Hugo satire (like Marie Duval's Ally Sloper stories) still misses fitting the crucial comic strip definition by its general lack of dialogue of any kind (Cham preferred satiric prose captions to each mute drawing) and its obvious movement toward a preordained conclusion.

Alfred de Musset's richly comic limning of the destruction of a rival lover's nose, in Rudolphe Töppfer's captioned panel-strip manner (1840).

Felix Tournachon's classic panel-strip satire on a reactionary politico, Mossieu Reac, in an 1848 excerpt.

A wonderfully funny pictorial work directed toward the authoritarian absurdities of the France of Napoleon III by another French cartoonist, Felix Tournachon (who drew and wrote as Nadar), called *Vie Publique et Privée de Mossieu Reac,* dealt with a reactionary politician whose activities paralleled those of the ruler of the Second Empire. Unhappily short-lived — the graphic serial was in effect suppressed by the regime — Nadar's work in the picture story format, as evidenced in this truncated work, might well have equaled Cham's if he had been able to continue.

Gustave Doré and Honoré Daumier did too little sustained work in pictorial narrative (weighed against their total output of art in other areas) to be considered in this brief overview — although Doré's early "Life in the Provinces" and similar quietly humorous japes, as well as his vitriolic narrative satire of 1854 on the absurdities and nastiness of Czarist Russian history (the latter impaired by a deliberately crude graphic technique apparently meant to resemble botched woodcuts and so reflect the crudities of Russian history and life), are certainly memorable work in themselves. Wilhelm Busch, on the other hand, probably Germany's greatest cartoonist, devoted virtually all of his creative graphic work of the 1860s and later to the picture story in many different lengths, eschewing single-panel gag and political cartoons almost altogether. There is no doubt that Busch made a finished art form of the picture story, moving from short slapstick anecdotes of three or four pages (all captioned with rhyming couplets) to longer narratives built around continuing characters, ultimately producing works of a considerable philosophic depth (without abandoning his basically humorous concepts) in greater continuous length and variability of pictorial format.

While there are stylistic elements in Busch's work that appear odd to the contemporary eye (notably the tendency of his figures to look like shapeless powdered dumplings, a comic graphic technique which was pursued elsewhere in nineteenth century

Honoré Daumier's memorable comic duo, Ratapoil and Casmajou, in a flamboyantly cocky pose from 1851.

Overview

Wilhelm Busch's famed demonic kids in a more playful moment from 1862: the pair, Max and Moritz, inspired the Katzenjammer Kids newspaper strips of the next century.

cartoon humor, to the best later effect in Marie Duval's Ally Sloper stories), the overall impact of Busch's rich narrative imagination and forceful pictorial statement compels us to read through page after page of his stories with no inclination to stop. While the stories themselves are often not especially funny to modern eyes, laden as they are with heavy provincial humor of the period, the art itself is endlessly risible.

Never far from the farmyard — Busch's characters and settings are almost invariably bucolic and peasant — the German artist's work frequently and uncritically reflects the casual brutality of life in such an environment, in sharp contrast to the humanistic urban orientation of most picture story productions of the time. This can, of course, be disturbing to more sensitive temperaments, then as now. In one story, "The Peashooter," an older man punishes a small boy who has been pestering him with peas and darts by seizing his peashooter, jamming it though the boy's teeth and deep into his throat, and leaving a last panel residue of broken teeth and dripping blood where the boy had been standing. And in Busch's classic work, the linked-story narrative of *Max and Moritz* (the demonic duo who would later be developed by German-American artist Rudolph Dirks as *The Katzenjammer Kids* in the U.S. Sunday newspaper comics), the purportedly comic goings-on are occasionally far too conceptually unpleasant to amuse us much now. Nevertheless, the wondrously deft drawings of the two boys and their adult victims here, as with all of Busch's enormous cast of kids, farmers, housewives and farm animals, are so unfailingly delightful that they override most qualms. Despite a further annoying tendency to violently kill off most of his major story characters at the end — the demise of a marvelous comic raven in "Hans Huckebein, the Unlucky Raven," is particularly hard to take — Busch's sunny art cavalierly dispels the narrative morbidity and leaves most readers with the rare and pleasant sense of having experienced a uniquely rewarding and memorable body of work.

Equally gifted with a marvelously funny style but much kinder to her characters (and the modern reader), the French cartoonist Marie Duval, who co-edited the weekly satirical magazine *Judy* with her English husband Charles H. Ross, drew several hundred picture stories during her stint on that cartoon journal from 1869 through 1877, a large part of which were devoted to the comic development of a classic rogue and swindler named Ally Sloper.

Still a byword in England today, Sloper's solitary and long-lasting fame is a literary and artistic oddity. Doctor Syntax made Rowlandson famous; Tom, Jerry, and Logic made the Cruikshanks famous; Pickwick, of course, did the same for Dickens and Phiz. Ally Sloper, however, made only Ally Sloper famous. Aside from a few people interested in nineteenth century cartoon art in general, no one recognizes the names of Duval and Ross, or of W. G. Baxter and R. W. Thomas, who carried the Sloper image to its greatest heights of popular appeal through the last two decades of the nineteenth century.

Sloper, in appearance a mixture of Phiz's Micawber from *David Copperfield* and (to contemporary eyes) a gleeful Walter Matthau, sported Micawber's battered top hat but replaced Micawber's jaunty walking stick with a shabby furled umbrella. His conniving, raffish behavior, largely limited to harmless swindles, petty thefts, and assorted crookery by his total lack of ambition and foresight, was thwarted rather than abetted by the ruinous proposals of his younger and not over-bright accomplice, Ikey Mo. It was the comic pretense of Duval's and Ross's narrative line that Sloper was a hanger-on at *Judy*'s offices who could not be gotten rid of and so was occasionally put to minimal use on "foreign" assignments to nearby points in Europe simply to keep him out of the way while he spent his stipend filing useless reports — which were, nonetheless, printed in *Judy* to the general delectation of the readers.

It was this jaunty issue-by-issue handling of the Sloper character, complete with tidbits of data about his comings and goings, coupled with printed anecdotes about his demands for a raise and reader demands for his dismissal as an imposition on their trust in *Judy*, that led eventually to the incredible (but documented) belief among a good part of London's cockney and working class populace that Sloper was a real person. Certainly the deluge of Sloper toys, dolls, antimacassars, albums, and what have you in the London shops of the 1870s and '80s could have led the credulous to believe that the source of all this bric-a-brac must actually exist.

Judy was in fact a cartoon weekly aimed at the younger, just-married members of the rising middle class (with a special slant toward the wives), and the saucy and lively tone it contrived to captivate these readers was in large part augmented by Marie Duval's lubriciously funny cartoon story pages about Sloper and other bizarre creations of her pen. Indeed, Duval's inspired rendering of Sloper in gamy action was usually much funnier than

A Chaplinesque pantomime panel-story sequence by Busch from the 1860s.

the story lines Ross wrote for her to illustrate, giving her more than a stylistic similarity to the Busch whose art also held viewers less than enchanted with his own narratives. From time to time, however, the Sloper stories could be delightfully inventive in themselves, and the reader wonders if Duval's hand was not at the helm on those occasions.

Calculatedly maladroit and careless (Duval would make a point, for example, of keeping her characters' faces out of plumb from one panel to the next), her work seems devised to reflect a no-nonsense, last-minute, pared-down spontaneity of concept and execution, dashed off with squinted eye and cornered tongue against a just-past deadline. Nothing much like her comically wretched style has been seen before or since (although a vestige of it can be found in World War II's universally anonymous "Kilroy was here!" graffiti, while Bud Grace's contemporary comic strip *Ernie*, sired by way of *The Bungle Family* and *Nize Baby* in tone, manner, and sloppy style, is today a solitary spiritual heir of Marie Duval's *Ally*); it is unique to her pen; and it is — *because* of its preposterous faults and flubs and the leaping comic life these somehow give her raffish array of characters — ineffably and forever funny.

Thus the comic strip, the major graphic media star of our time, was kept waiting in the wings of the nineteenth century to be led on stage at last in full, final format by the grimy hand of the Yellow Kid for a brief, little noted bow in October of 1896, to be followed by a handful of similarly short, little glimpsed turns with the Kid and Rudy Dirks' just-born Katzenjammer Kids, until its engagement in a major comic-page production by a far-sighted Fred Opper in 1900, called *Happy Hooligan*, where the strip's innovative dialogue balloons were waved like flags in every panel week after week, to lead finally to wild national appreciation and applause — and to the sincerest possible form of approbation, virtually universal imitation for the whole of the new century. The remainder of these volumes will be devoted to a long and detailed look at the new narrative form's remarkable performance through the ensuing hundred years. Enjoy. You can't help it.

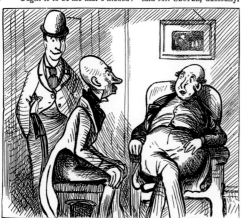

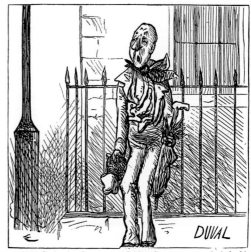

A slapstick captioned panel-story by Marie Duval for *Judy*, featuring her classic comic characters, Ally Sloper and Ikey Mo (1871).

THE WINDOW SHIVERED AS SPRING-HEELED JACK LEAPED BODILY THROUGH IT.

A bizarre cartoon illustration for *Spring-Heeled Jack*, a weekly pennydreadful parts-issue magazine of circa 1860. Jack was the first dual-identity costumed crime-fighter in English fiction. Author, artist anonymous.

Richard Prowse's rousing cartoon plate of 1861 for George Augustus Sala's *Charley Wag*, a penny-blood parts-issue about London slum life; like *Jack* a classic of its kind.

Overview

TWO | 1900–1929

BALLOONING WITH THE WIZARDS OF HAWKS
How the New Art and Its Practitioners Stripped the Gears of the National Media and Ruled the Newsprint Roost From 1900 Through 1929

In the first three decades of that freshly unleashed art form, the comic strip, comedy was king.

Fred Opper introduced *Alphonse and Gaston* and *Maud* to play pranks in the Hearst comics with *Happy Hooligan,* which they did for most of the next thirty years. Jimmy Swinnerton trained into Manhattan from San Francisco, leaving the odd and funny *Little Bears* feature he had started in Hearst's *Examiner* there and giving life to a short-lived strip called *Little Tigers* for Hearst's morning *New York Journal,* dropping it to start his long-lived and hugely popular *Jimmy* page by 1902. (Swinnerton was the first "funny animal" artist in the strips; his *Examiner* bears had reflected the state flag of California, as his tigers played with the once notorious New York Tammany tiger of Thomas Nast.) Rudy Dirks kicked his earlier *Katzenjammer Kids* (largely a captioned-panel and pantomime page in the 1890s) into full comic strip gear, adding the unhappy boarder named Der Captain and the shanghaied truant officer named Der Inspector to Mama K's bedeviled menage within the first decade of the classic strip.

To compound the fun, Hearst introduced black and white strips to his daily editorial pages, then expanded them into his sports and classified-ad pages, building toward the first full-page array of daily strips in the 1912 *New York Evening Journal* (a second daily he had started in the 1890s). The publisher had even, without thinking of it as anything special, managed to publish the first daily comic strip, ever, in the same paper in 1898 — nothing less than a daily *Yellow Kid* strip!)

Other newspaper publishers, startled into action by the joyous public reception of the new strip form in the Hearst papers, launched some comic cruisers of their own, replete with full color bunting and captained by old and new strip talents.

Outcault, bereft of his fabled Yellow Kid due to the hysteric American revulsion toward anything of a yellow hue during the Spanish-American war (the flag of Spain, it seems, had a yellow band in it), returned to the Sunday page fray with a new winner, *Buster Brown,* for the *New York Herald.* (Later, Outcault and Buster were to be scooped up by — of course — the Hearst papers.)

Working for the Philadelphia papers, newcomers Charles W. Kahles and George Herriman undertook a series of popular strips, notably Kahles' *Hairbreadth Harry* and Herriman's *Major Ozone, The Fresh Air Fiend,* which soon entered the national strip syndication sweepstakes together with the knockout Hearst package. (Herriman did a freelance daily strip for Hearst's *Los Angeles Examiner* which developed into his famous *Krazy Kat* of later years; Kahles resisted the Hearst invitations until his death in 1930, living quite well off the proceeds of his popular Harry, Belinda, and Rudolph Rassendale epic.

In Chicago, the *Tribune* published the first newspaper "answer" to parent and church groups' fussing over lowbrow and brutal slapstick elements in the color comics (led by a fiercely editorializing *Ladies' Home Journal*), *The Kin-Der-Kids* by famed German magazine cartoonist Lyonel Feininger. The *New York Herald* followed with Winsor McCay's idyllic fantasy *Little Nemo in Slumberland.* Both quickly turned to lowbrow slapstick themselves to hold their audience as newspaper circulation slipped after their introduction.

Humor was the clear keynote of all these early strips, as it was of their companions and successors through the 1920s: even with the introduction of nominal suspense as early as Opper's *Alphonse and Gaston* in 1903, it was always burlesque suspense, while the continuity which developed strongly in the daily strips a few years later was based on satiric and familial story lines, never serious menace or even romance.

(The single — and very curious — exception to this pattern was a brief half-page Sunday strip which appeared in the *Chicago Tribune* in 1902, called *Hugo Hercules* and drawn by one J. Koerner, a work which has to be called the first serious superhero strip; it was perfectly straightforward and not funny at all, a genuine oddity of the time.)

The comedy itself ranged across the spectrum of possibilities, from the murderously (and hilariously) brutal *Mutt and Jeff* of Bud Fisher, through the comically suspenseful race track problems of *Barney Google*, the battlefield marriage of Maggie and Jiggs in *Bringing Up Father,* the family obstacle courses of *Their Only Child* and *Toots and Casper,* the bizarre domestic fantasy of *Polly and Her Pals* (in which, despite the title, Paw Perkins, the cat and valet are the chief characters), the conniving con-artist antics of *Joe and Asbestos,* the fanciful railway station moonshine of *Jerry on the Job*, the Prohibition nose-thumbing and rowdy raillery of *Moon Mullins,* the quiet day-to-day family growth of *Gasoline Alley,* the mad soap opera pursuit of riches in *The Gumps,* and the taboo-taunting triumvirate of Ham Gravy and Castor and Olive Oyl in *Thimble Theatre* (which was to give tormented birth to Popeye in 1929), to the first effective comic-page adaptation of a cinema star in *Felix the Cat*.

Unlike the popular acceptance of cartoon art in the mid-nineteenth century as a vehicle for any subject from murder to pathos, the general public of the 1890s and later had come to associate cartoon art solely with gag panels, political satire, and narrative humor. A serious strip adaptation of, say, Sherlock Holmes would have been out of the question in the minds of editors, publishers and artists alike. Even the logical transferral of dime novel action narratives to strips, aside from the prevailing onus the dime and nickel books carried with public authorities, would have been conceptually beyond the pale, which is too bad: daily continuity strips featuring Nick Carter, Old Sleuth, Old and Young King Brady, Buffalo Bill, Young Wild West, Frank Reade or Deadwood Dick — there were even Calamity Jane dimes — would have formed a marvelous period contrast with the otherwise universally comic work in the strips.

Even when serious death-dealing, action-suspense narrative did haltingly touch tepid toe to cold syndicate waters in the mid-1920s, there was no little public dismay and complaint (which the broad range of editors found it safe to dismiss only a few years further on, after the action strips had demonstrated their strong ability to build circulation and attract advertisers by the early 1930s).

So comedy ruled for over a quarter of a century after 1900, and had only partly yielded space to the serious story strips by the mid-1930s. But this die was cast from the first, when the newspaper color comic sections of the 1890s opted to imitate the gag cartoon magazines of the period in layout and comic graphic content. Here, also, low comedy was all.

In these popular cartoon weeklies — *Life, Puck, Judge* and *Truth* were among the most noted titles — the "book" was built around a weekly full-page (or larger) political cartoon, which was the nominal reason for the magazine's existence, and which got them into the homes of the well-to-do due to the largely conservative bias of these often masterful cartoons. (The *Puck* political cartoonist through much of this period was Fred Opper.) A certain amount of light, humorous text made up of comic anecdotes, fiction and reviews of books and plays surrounded the remainder of the cartoon graphic content, which was almost entirely gag cartoons and balloonless narratives.

This established format also came to prevail in the newspaper Sunday comic sections of the *World* and the *Journal,* thus continuing to mold the prevailing public view that what appeared in the magazines and the two newspapers comprised virtually all of the graphic possibilities of cartoon art, apart from children's book and humorous book illustration.

Prominent among the gag cartoon themes of the time (which included rube farmers, bicyclists, ethnic stereotypes, saloons, girls and beaux, commuters, well-off kids and their governesses, motor cars, trolleys and funny animals) was the antic behavior of the slum kids, particularly Irish slum kids. The reigning master of cartoon work in this area, who combined pathos and wit in his kid gag panels, was Michael Angelo Woolf, but a young and close imitator of Woolf's comic handling of his kids had emerged by 1893, appearing primarily in *Truth*, but also occasionally in the 1894 Sunday comic pages of the *World*.

Some of newcomer Richard Felton Outcault's work dealt with other subjects, notably clowns — his first color cartoon narrative, a pantomime piece, was a clown gag he drew for the *World* in 1894, titled (amusingly, in view of what he was to produce in October, 1896), "Origin of a New Species" — but his kid cartoon series, rougher and more broadly funny than most of Woolf's, made a hit with the *World* comic section editor and its readers.

Taking a hint from one or two other slum kid cartoonists, Outcault made his kids the residents of one or another particular neighborhood in the Manhattan Irish ghetto, chiefly for the comic effect of the names involved. (Some of the names used by Outcault and others were real, some invented.) After dealing with several such names, the new cartoonists settled on a fictional Hogan's Alley as a permanent setting for his gang, and as a running title for his large captioned panels, which the *World* had begun to print in color on a more or less weekly basis by 1895.

By then, an odd, jug-eared, nightshirted, barefoot tagalong kid had begun to show up on the sidelines of gang activities in the panels. Although essentially a comic background figure for a while (as he'd first appeared in a *Truth* cartoon early in 1895), the kid took the public fancy almost at once. Letters came in; associates commented happily about the goofy little guy to the editor and to Outcault himself, and fairly quickly the bat-eared kid became directly involved in the gang's derring-do. Then — suddenly — it was apparent that he had himself taken charge of the Hogan's Alley activities, zestfully egging the other kids on as he grinned out at his public and made oblique comments to *World* readers in gamely misspelled words lettered on his nightshirt, which Outcault had made into a spiffy dialogue balloon for the kid — amusing in itself but largely irrelevant to the panoramic riot going on behind him. The shy little gink in the rear of the Alley gang had become the wildly popular (and popularly named) Yellow Kid, the color of his nightshirt — earlier green and red — now having become a permanent glaring yellow.

The Yellow Kid (or Mickey Dugan, as Outcault christened him) became the first continuing star of a newspaper comic section almost overnight, virtually eclipsing the more carefully nurtured weekly appeal of the *World*'s color-section political cartoon by Walt MacDougall, to say nothing of the *World*'s elaborately written and illustrated Sunday magazine section, with its circus-poster art stories on man-eating trees in Bolivia and art-model murders in evil Paris. On Sunday, if you ponied up your nickel for the *World,* it was the carnival kid you were really paying for — the irresistible candied cherry that *had* to be ingested before the rest of the tasty sundae could be tackled.

Not that the *World* wasn't a hell of a journalistic sundae the rest of the week as well. It had, in fact, built its enormous New York City sales and considerable national circulation *on* cartoons from the 1880s on, filling its daily and Sunday news columns with small column-wide cartoon cuts (largely drawn by MacDougall) of individuals and events that had to be followed in other papers through unrelieved gray masses of text. As quickly as they could, most Manhattan dailies followed the *World*'s lead in illustrated news stories, but the *World* had long since seized the public interest and built on it with an electrifying illustrated Sunday paper that battened on lengthy accounts of sensational news of all kinds.

When this device was followed by the *World*'s acquisition of one of the first mass-production color presses ever bought by a newspaper, and the resultant production of eight pages of partially colored Sunday cartoon art headed each week by a full-color MacDougall political cartoon meant to be clipped and posted in barber shops and saloons as free *Herald* advertising, there seemed to be no limit to the paper's soaring readership (even in the immigrant ghettos, where the *World*'s abundant pictures and cartoons proved a pleasant aid to learning English). Adding the ebullient Yellow Kid to this volatile mix simply popped the top of the circulation thermometer.

A monied newspaper publisher a continent away in San Francisco had watched all this with fascination and a fast-growing belief that — with his parent's millions — he could buy a New York newspaper and tackle the *World* head-on for circulation. All he had to do, after all, was buy out the *World*'s talent and sell it to New York readers under the aegis of *his* newspaper. So William Randolph Hearst came to Manhattan in 1895, bought the moribund *New York Journal* (itself already a desperately striving imitation of the *World*, chockfull of rowdy comic art and sensational news stories), and took on the *World*.

In short order, Hearst bought and installed Manhattan's second newsprint color press, hired away the best of the *World*'s staff of editors, writers and artists, added additional top talent from around the city, and by the fall of 1896 had launched his own color comic section, featuring — who else? — Outcault's Yellow Kid in all of his toothy, barefoot, brazenly vulgar glory. The *World* gamely fought back, fielding their own Yellow Kid as drawn by a new young cartoonist named George B. Luks, but it was no contest: the Luks Kid was sloppy and silly in execution and behavior, while Hearst gave his readers not just one but two (count 'em, two) *Yellow Kid* cartoons each week as drawn by the Kid's inspired creator himself.

(It should be noted here that Hearst even had the edge in nomenclature: he'd had the good sense to use the public's common name for the *World*'s *Hogan's Alley* hero for *his* Outcault work, while the *World*, which had oddly never used the "Yellow Kid" term in its pages, holding to the *Hogan's Alley* series title alone, was stuck with the latter name in promoting its Luks feature, leaving Hearst free to splash posters everywhere proclaiming the *Journal*'s ownership of Outcault *and* the Yellow Kid.)

Hearst's *Journal* circulation soon leapfrogged to match the *World*'s, and then surpassed it, with many New Yorkers buying both papers every Sunday to read the lavish color comic sections and sensational news spreads which both now featured in toe-to-toe competition.

Meanwhile, the publishers of other major newspapers around the country had viewed the power of the new color comic sections with a mixture of horror and awe — and hastened to try out their own versions as soon as they could invest in color presses. From Los Angeles to Chicago to Philadelphia, locally edited and drawn color comic sections blossomed between 1897 and 1900, usually limited to four pages and consisting wholly of humorous text and an array of comic pictures often drawn by barely competent high school and college talent (since skilled professional cartoonists were in short supply away from Manhattan). Some papers attempted to develop continuing comic figures like Outcault's Kid without much apparent success, but the public responded as expected to the extra Sunday treats by ballooning the sales of the innovative papers.

Thus a ready national market was established several years in advance of the syndicating of "name" comic strips that would be initiated by Hearst and others shortly after the turn of the century, once Opper had shown the True Path to fame and fortune in cartoon art with his nailing down of the classic comic strip format in *Happy Hooligan*.

The daily comic strip developed later and along a notably different path than the more glamorous Sunday color page. Its real appeal to circulation-minded newspaper publishers lay in its easy accessibility to six-day-a-week afternoon newspapers, sold largely to inner-city workers and suburban commuters for reading directly after work and concerned chiefly with stock market results and crime and sports news. Calling for no color press outlay and taking up only a quarter to an eighth of a page apiece, daily comic strips could be sandwiched into the rear pages of such papers, among the classified ad listings and the sports and theatrical news.

Daily strips held less appeal for morning papers which already had color comic sections on Sunday; in fact, many such papers ran only one daily strip (or none at all) for nearly a decade into the new century, feeling that the family readership for which the morning papers aimed would find them vulgar and intrusive in the actual news pages, rather than relegated to a special section of their own as they were on Sundays. Here, as in so many other areas of strip development, Hearst was the first to break away from the prevailing rule, and daily strips flooded into his morning papers across the country after 1915.

The first comic strip to appear for a number of successive days anywhere was Outcault's *Yellow Kid* work for Hearst's *Evening Journal* in 1898, where it was literally drawn and printed from day to day to parallel the U.S. invasion of Cuba (the Kid and his gang staging their own "invasion" in tandem with the American forces). With its continued narrative and in-panel dialogue balloon exchange among the characters, the Outcault daily reflected the accidental strip innovation which historically emerged in his Sunday Yellow Kid narratives of October 1896 and later.

After a week and a half, with the Kid and his cronies declaring a total victory and making merry with the "liberated" Cuban ladies, the evening newspaper strip vanished, with nothing of the sort to be seen until 1904 when a Hearst editor for the *Chicago Evening American* asked Clare Briggs, the paper's staff cartoonist, to undertake a quasi-daily sports-page strip about a down-at-the-heels pony player to be called, after its tacky hero, *A. Piker Clerk*. The real gimmick of the strip, however, was not its incidental slapstick humor, but the more or less daily racetrack tips the artist worked into Clerk's hazardous betting activities. After this then-bizarre work had appeared for a few months (without ever quite hitting a real day-to-day publication routine), Hearst noticed it from his offices in New York and ordered it squashed as vulgar — not because of its raffish comedy but because of the providing of track suggestions which had the effect of making the *American* a tipsheet.

Obviously inspired by Briggs' 1904 "A. Piker Clerk" experiment, Bud Fisher, a young sports-page cartoonist for the *San Francisco Chronicle,* talked his editor into letting him take a crack at the same idea in a daily strip to carry the name "A. Mutt." First seen by doubtless startled racetrack bettors on November 15, 1907, under the strip-long title "Mr. A. Mutt Starts in to Play the Races," another desperately obsessed horseplayer, with the same lean and hungry look that had characterized Briggs' Clerk, rushed from tipster to track clutching a handful of rent money to put on the nose of a very long shot day after day. Many of Mutt's long shots paid off; many did not, but the readers seemed to get a kick out of the new gimmick (and a solid laugh out of Fisher's comic rendering of his loss-beleaguered hero), and the circulation of the *Chronicle* jumped noticeably, to the detriment of its chief competitor, Hearst's *San Francisco Examiner*.

Apprised of this problem, Hearst became less concerned with nominal vulgarity and more worried over the newsstand beating his West Coast paper was taking. "Buy Fisher" came over the wire, and in short order A. Mutt's boss was working for the *Examiner* sports editor. A cautious fellow, Fisher mailed a couple of his last strip episodes to Washington; unnoticed by Hearst, they carried "Copyright H. C. Fisher" notices when they hit print. This didn't prevent the *Chronicle* from hiring another cartoonist to continue an "A. Mutt" strip for its sport page, but Fisher, amused at the hectic competition and in any event a friend of the new artist, Russ Westover (in later years to be famed for *Tillie the Toiler*), made no issue of his legal control of the character at the time. Westover's A. Mutt crashed and died in a year or so (in fact, Westover had his Mutt commit suicide at the end), while Fisher's gamy gambler grabbed back the lost *Examiner* circulation in no time. Impressed, Hearst put Fisher under a national syndication contract in 1909 and trained him to Manhattan to pursue A. Mutt's career in a straight gag-a-day strip.

The success of this first prolonged daily strip was not lost on other cartoonists, and George Herriman began work on three different daily strips for *his* sports editor on Hearst's *Los Angeles Examiner*, as did a number of other artists on various newspapers between 1908 and 1910. Herriman's strip work, especially his last effort on the Los Angeles paper, *Gooseberry Sprigg* (which managed to introduce — on the sidelines, like Outcault's Kid — a fey, tail-twisting black kat named Krazy), got him a Hearst train ticket to New York in 1910, after which Herriman set syndication sail with his famed *Family Upstairs* daily strip.

(In the meantime, Fisher had placed sharper focus on a sometimes-buddy of A. Mutt's, a lunatic asylum inmate who fancied himself to be James J. Jeffries, the famed prize fighter, calling him Jeff for short; and the strip's name became *Mutt and Jeff* at last.)

Between 1910 and 1915, the six-day-a-week daily strip proliferated. (Prior to those dates, many weekday strips ran erratically, from two to four but almost never six days a week, primarily in the various Hearst newspapers.) Among the growing multitude of strips that took root in afternoon dailies then were *Us Boys*, a witty suburban kid comic adventure strip; *Desperate Desmond*, a Harry Hershfield spoof of stage melodrama similar to Kahles' Sunday *Hairbreadth Harry*; Cliff Sterrett's surreal *Polly and Her Pals* in an inspired daily version; the unnamed daily epic featuring Krazy Kat and Ignatz Mouse, which ran the lower length of *The Family Upstairs* in its own set of fast-action panels; *Sherlocko the Monk*, the titular culmination of Gus Mager's series of "Monk" dailies (featuring such Irish-ape characters as Henpecko the Monk, Tightwaddo the Monk and Groucho the Monk, and incidentally, serving as the source of the Marx Brothers' stage names); *Colonel Heeza Liar* and *Farmer Al Falfa*, early short-lived strip spinoffs of animated cartoons; *Brainy Bowers and Drowsy Duggan*, an early slapstick oddity that only latterly hit the six-day standard; *The Outbursts of Everett True*, the long-running panel strip whose irascible hero inspired Fontaine Fox's classic "Terrible-Tempered Mr. Bang" in *Toonerville Folks*, another early panel strip, that moved — like *Henry*, *Skippy*, and *The Little King* decades later — from the pages of a popular magazine into the newspapers; *The Hall-Room Boys*, the first bachelor-buddies strip, with a wry urban humor years ahead of its time; and Swinnerton's *Mr. Jack*, about a philandering comic tiger and his vengeful wife, the final wrapup of the Tammany Tigers Sunday page of 1901.

By the 1920s, of course, the tidal lift of daily strips had filled full pages of virtually every paper in the country, morning or evening. Generally speaking, the morning papers, going into homes, featured family and kid strips, while the afternoon racetrack and crime dailies were rife with lowbrow characters and con artists, their strip heroes reflecting the regular inhabitants of their news pages. The a.m. gazettes rolled with *Bringing Up Father*, *Toots and Casper*, *Tillie the Toiler*, *Skippy*, *Gus and Gussie*, *Sappo* (then a commuter strip), *The Gumps*, *Winnie Winkle*, *Harold Teen*, and their ilk. The p.m. sheets rocked with *Thimble Theatre*, *Everett True*, *Abie the Agent*, *Nize Baby*, *Moon Mullins*, *Barney Google* (which was, however, on the sports pages of Hearst morning papers), *Hairbreadth Harry*, *The Bungle Family*, *Jerry on the Job*, and *Toonerville Folks*, as well as the tentative trial balloons for the adventure strips that were to nearly dominate the comics in the 1930s and later: *Phil Hardy*, *Little Orphan Annie*, *Minute Movies*, *Wash Tubbs*, *Bobby Thatcher*, and, a good deal later in the decade, *Connie*, *Buck Rogers*, *Tarzan*, *Scorchy Smith*, *Tailspin Tommy*, and *Broncho Bill*.

With American newspapers packed fore and aft with comic strips by the end of the 1920s, the graphic scene was set for the great newspaper strip competition of the 1930s, with the eight-page Sunday comic sections of the preceding decade exploding into 16-page and 32-page extravaganzas, and single pages of daily comics doubling and even tripling in extent, with every small-town paper in the country adding a Saturday or Sunday comic section, often amounting to 16 tabloid pages in black and white — anything and everything to keep a depression-wracked populace buying newspapers.

And it worked!

THREE | 1930–1939

FROM ROUGH HOUSE'S CAFE TO MONGO
The Rocketship Ascent of Newspaper Comics in the Decade of the Scarce Dime (Or, "Brother, Can You Spare the Sunday Funnies?")

Ka-whoppity-thump!

The Sunday newspaper of the 1930s, rainbow-wrapped in laughter, and given a heart outfielder's throw from a car or bicycle pausing in the gray dawn outside, has arrived! Waiting juvenile hands scooped up the fat sausage of newsprint that had just been delivered and carried it inside to still-warm waiting beds or to kitchen tables where bowls of Post Toasties and milk, half eaten during the wait for the six a.m. arrival of the Sunday funnies, were polished off as *Flash Gordon* or *Tarzan* or *Mickey Mouse* were devoured by eager, wide-awake eyes.

The great Sunday morning ritual of the Depression Thirties, devoutly carried out once a week by American kids, had been born of dire necessity — the vital need of kids across the country to set the Sunday funnies read and digested along with cereal and milk *before* the bleary-eyed adults in the families got to them, hogging them for what could seem like *hours*...for the weekend color comics, once routinely tossed to the kids in the 1920s and before, had grabbed the rapt attention of millions of adults nationwide in the 1930s.

Although grown-up strip narrative and graphic realism in comics had been waiting in the wings from the mid-1920s in such daily strips as Roy Crane's *Wash Tubbs*, J. R. Williams' triple-narrative *Out Our Way*, Frank Godwin's *Connie*, and Harold Foster's text-and-panel *Tarzan of the Apes*, the majority of American newspapers had ignored the new development away from slapstick and broad satire, sticking with their long-established certainty that comics, daily and (particularly) Sunday, were *lagniappe* for the family kids. That all changed with the stock market crash of 1929 and an ensuing sharp drop in the subscription circulation of newspapers everywhere. Income-pinched heirs of the Great Depression cut back on what had been considered normal daily expenses in every way possible, including newspapers.

Once the reality of the long-term likelihood of a belt-tightened America had set in, however, people began to reconsider their options, particularly in the realm of entertainment, since at least occasional escape from the daily round of poverty came to seem vital. Sensing this conflict of choice between movies, magazines — in a pre-paperback era, books were out of the question as likely entertainment purchases — and newspapers (radio was a given: cheap sets were already in virtually every home), the big newspaper publishers and feature syndicates decided to make a strong pitch for the *adult* audiences, the people who actually spent the scarce family fun money, and backed the introduction of serious action adventure and crime comics to entice exactly these people to pay active personal attention to the daily and (particularly) the Sunday comics.

The graphic glamour and exciting novelty of such new color pages as *Buck Rogers, Tarzan, Tailspin Tommy,* and similar features, backed up by adult woman-directed humor in pages such as *Ella Cinders, Dixie Dugan, Tillie the Toiler* and the like, coupled with the often gripping story hooks of a flash flood of daily suspense action and soap strips that enlivened the back pages of weekday newspapers for the new target audiences, brought an entertainment-starved national focus on the old, gag-oriented comic pages — and got the pennies and nickels rolling out of American pockets for newspapers once again. Needless to say, the family kids hardly felt shut out of the new comic-page excitement; they were enthralled by science fiction, jungle adventure, and cops versus crime in the funnies. Now the entire family wanted to read comics every day, and particular Sunday.

From the perspective of the 1990s, with its myriad electronic diversions, it can understandably be more than a little difficult to imagine a time just over a half century ago when sixteen-page Sunday comic sections could be a wildly welcome high point of weekend entertainment at home, holding a rainy or winter-day family together until Jack Benny and Fred Allen cracked millions up at nightfall on the universal home radio sets. But as the pages of this collection make clear, the extraordinary newspaper comic strips of the 1930s were different from anything we have seen in papers over the past forty years.

For in these strips, and for the last time on a broad scale, humor and dramatic narrative were fully developed through careful, detailed art framed in strip panels as large as book illustrations, and set forth in sufficient dialogue exchange to establish sustained dramatic tension and to display character in depth, in a manner found today only well away from newspapers, in good graphic novels and some continuing-character comic books. First-rate strip narrative appeared in dozens of these attention-grabbing comics of the 1930s; let's take a deep mental breath and let a squadron or two of the vanished great roll in review —

Buck Rogers and *Tarzan* led the way for the sudden incursion of bizarre adventure action into the comics, followed by a set of imaginative and graphically riveting crime and detection strips in the wake of *Dick Tracy*'s probing yellow fedora: *Dan Dunn, The Shadow, Radio Patrol, Red Barry, Secret Agent X-9*, and a cluster of lesser lights; women in roles of assertive power flourished in *Connie, Myra North, Jane Arden*, and *Orphan Annie*; the ramshackle, rattling excitement of crate aviation roared in with *Tailspin Tommy, Flying to Fame, Skyroads*, and a comically exciting set of nose-diving sky adventures in *Mickey Mouse*; high comedy reigned in the family-life soaps, from *The Gumps, Toots and Casper* and *The Nebbs* to *Boots and Her Buddies, Polly and Her Pals* and *The Bungle Family* (where time-travel and extraterrestrials got into the grandly funny act); grim Depression realism seeped around the edges of the working-girl strips, *Dixie Dugan, Fritzi Ritz, Winnie Winkle, Ella Cinders, Olly of the Movies*, and even the highly fanciful *Somebody's Stenog*; comic characters got delightfully involved in genuinely suspenseful adventures in *Thimble Theatre Starring Popeye, The Captain and the Kids, Danny Dingle, Boob McNutt, Looy Dot Dope, Ming Foo, Mickey Finn, Hairbreadth Harry* and *Ally Opp*; roistering soldier-of-fortune adventure flashed death-dealing swords in *Wash Tubbs, Captain Easy, Scorchy Smith, Terry and the Pirates* and *Dickie Dare*; kids took the home-town high ground in *Skippy, Henry, Nipper, Cap Stubbs, Elmer, Freckles and His Friends* and *The Katzenjammer Kids*; twee lunacy opened asylums of fun in *Smokey Stover, The Squirrel Cage, Hejji, The Little King, Hoosegow Herman, Colonel Potterby and the Duchess, Dave's Delicatessen, Count Screwloose, Bunky* and *Brutus*; ray guns, rockets, and a giant gyro tilted to throw the earth off its axis ushered science fiction in with *Flash Gordon, Jack Swift, Don Dixon and the Hidden Empire, Sappo, Superman* and (from 1938 on) *Connie*; empty saddles in the old corral marked a dearth of hard-riding Westerns in the 1930s, and only *Bronc Peeler, Broncho Bill, Little Joe* and *White Boy* were memorable; affable family life ambled quietly along in *Gasoline Alley* and exploded occasionally into rampaging puppies and trampled mailmen in *Blondie*, slumping into lethargy in *Mr. and Mrs.*, but enlivened with bombast and chicanery in *Our Boarding House* and *Room and Board*; old-time slapstick thrived in *That's My Pop, Mutt and Jeff, Needlenose Noonan, Lena Pry, Peter Rabbit*, much of *Minute Movies, Felix the Cat, Napoleon, Lala Palooza, Cicero's Cat, Betty Boop, Dinglehoofer and His Dog, Donald Duck* and *Big Chief Wahoo*; jug-fresh mountain music (and mountain dew) went into three hillbilly classics, *Li'l Abner, The Mountain Boys* and *Barney Google* after 1934, plus seminal sequences in the prize-fighting strip *Joe Palooka*; and under-used historic adventure found a bourne only in *Prince Valiant*, the nicely-drawn but inconsequential *Peter Pat*, Will Eisner's *Hawks of the Seas* (intended for newspaper use), and about a third of the stories in the bizarre anthology strip *Minute Movies*. Going its own sweet, serene way through all of this — and kept by public incomprehension into only two Sunday newspapers — was, of course, the best strip of all (and of all time, for that matter), George Herriman's inimitable and timeless *Krazy Kat*.

It was a stunning roster of imaginative and graphic accomplishment, an apogee of an art, both in quality and quantity. As the newspaper wars for readership heated up by the mid-1930s, Sunday comic sections expanded to as much as 24 pages in full newspaper-page size and to as much as 36 pages in tabloid format, with new strips being rushed into print to supply the fresh demand. Many of these ranged from passably entertaining to downright dreadful, and soon slipped out of sight virtually without notice. But in general the fierce demand for first-rate new syndicate product brought an inordinate amount of real comic strip talent to light, launching dozens of successful careers for such newcomers to the field as Al Capp, Alex Raymond, Chester Gould, Harold Foster, Burne Hogarth, Dr. Seuss, Bill Freyse, Milton Caniff, O. Soglow, Chic Young, a renovated E. C. Segar, Bill Holman, Fred Harman, Floyd Gottfredson, and a host of others literally too numerous to list.

Unfortunately, the panel space necessary to sustain work of such quality was swiftly and brutally reduced, not once but again and again in World War II and the years following, as half the newspapers in the country succumbed to new home and commuter reading patterns and the impact of television, and the cluster of remaining strips fought for space in the papers that survived. By the 1960s, the newspapers' need for quantity of strips had triumphed almost entirely over any serious interest in quality of story line or art.

But there *was* a great and fiercely creative epoch of strip work once, restructured here for a deprived generation of readers to relish and return to — with or without a bowl of corn flakes and the chill of a cold kitchen morning — again and again through the closing years of this memorable comic strip century. We'll never see its like again.

FOUR | 1940–1995

THE BLITZING AND BELITTLING OF THE COMICS
How Terry Left the Pirates to Go to War, Strip Readers were Orwellianly Instructed, Less is More, and There was no National Recovery Act for Comics

For a brief time at the beginning of the 1940s, it looked as if things were going to keep getting better for comics in the new decade. The tough battle for newspaper sales that had sustained strip development in the 1930s was still raging unabated, and took fresh, exciting fuel from a new notion that had suddenly emerged from the Chicago journalistic war front.

When the *Chicago Tribune*'s new and well-funded competitor the *Chicago Sun* not only introduced its own color comic section with an attractive array of new syndicated strip titles, but added an exciting innovative fresh concept in a 16-page comic-book-sized *Spirit* section edited and drawn by Will Eisner and his comic art associates, the *Tribune* felt forced to scramble for an answer in a similar section of its own called, without much imagination, *Comic Book Magazine*. Initially made up of a bizarre array of never-published strips from the 1920s and earlier by such *Tribune* stalwarts as Frank King and Ferd Johnson, the *Comic Book Magazine* quickly picked up a new crew of cartoonists, turning out strips which the *Tribune* made available to other newspapers only as a printed unit, just as the *Spirit* distributors were doing with their own magazine.

Thus virtually overnight the new *Sun* newspaper added a half dozen comics of its own to the national array, plus the three strips that made up *The Spirit* section, while the *Tribune* wound up throwing nearly a dozen new strip titles into the newsprint pot. On top of this, yet another new paper in New York, the tabloid *PM*, developed three new strips, including the nationally popular *Barnaby and Mr. O'Malley*, so that it seemed for a time — European war or no European war — that the golden comic strip age the Depression had ushered in was going to keep right on enlarging itself indefinitely.

Unhappily, in an augury of the real future, the old *Philadelphia Evening Ledger*, the long-standing showcase for the Ledger Syndicate's lineup of daily strips, threw in the towel and folded in November of 1941, just weeks before Pearl Harbor would see Americans buying every newspaper they could get their hands on for months and years to come — and with it, shortly thereafter, its classic set of titles, from *Connie* and *Hairbreadth Harry* to *Somebody's Stenog* and *The Shadow*, vanished from the syndication market forever. The first sizable victim in the long, slow attrition of American afternoon papers, the *Evening Ledger* was not immediately followed by other such journals only because of the huge boost America's entry into the war gave all newspapers over the next five years.

(The *Tribune*'s *Comic Book Magazine* itself failed to make it through the war. Torpedoed by insufficient syndication sales in 1943, its set of strips — highly popular in Chicago — were dumped into the already overloaded Sunday *Tribune* comic section. Further space reductions finished them off for good, except for two hardy survivors, *Brenda Starr* and *Texas Slim and Dirty Dalton*, which remained *Tribune* regulars for years to come. Buoyed by a broad syndication base, *The Spirit* continued entertaining its loyal readers until the 1950s.)

1943 was, in fact, the crunch year for the 1930s strips. The pre-war 16-page sections were chopped to eight and twelve pages, and full-page strips vanished for good from national print, except for King Features' highly prized *Prince Valiant* and *Bringing Up Father* pages, while at least three devoted papers nursed the Hogarth *Tarzan* through the war in its full size. Full-page formats were now to be found (if intermittently) only in the tabloid comic sections, while half-pages became standard for virtually all comics in full-sized sections. (Most of the third-page toppers introduced in the late 1920s to accompany famous King Features strips and others continued to appear in that format, but often widely separated from the features they had previously headed, while lesser strips in general were routinely cut to third-page size for publication.) Despite the wartime reduction in newsprint, the same number of ads were published as before, further crowding the remaining strips into more and more cramped corners. (One demented newspaper, the *San Francisco Chronicle*, routinely cut the bottom panel rows of many strips in half to accommodate small page-wide ads, leaving only a row of balloons and severed heads to be seen.) But it was all very patriotic and for a vital cause and the public made no complaint, little knowing that things would never change back.

Still, new strips continued to appear, old favorites continued, and the national adult love affair with the comics which the 1930s had engendered kept plenty of popular attention riveted to even the most severely downsized strips. (The dailies, of course, had also undergone a marked size reduction; pleased with the additional space gained, of course, most papers simply crowded in a few new titles, approaching the postage-stamp rows of today's daily comics.) But over the long haul in the post-war decades, the small size formats failed to hold the attention of the public. Realistic adventure and science fiction strips in which the glamour of detail was vital had become dark, squeezed blobs in the dailies and color-heavy rows of balloon-weighted panels in the Sundays, where even a fraction of off-register color printing (common in the post-war years) could ruin the readability of such works. More simplistic works fared a bit better (Chester Gould's clean-lined *Dick Tracy* held readers longer than many other pre-war favorites), but even here the surrender of balloon space to permit enough art to attract the public eye led to a lessening of exactly the dialogue sophistication which had originally earned the 1930s strips their new adult audience.

Appalled, a few doughty artists simply said the hell with it, and relied on a core audience of understanding readers to hold with their minutely-lettered balloons and intricately detailed art — a vocal audience which often was able to bully newspapers into giving such strips as *Pogo* and *Li'l Abner* pre-war size on the daily page, much as *Doonesbury* and *Calvin and Hobbes* claim in some papers today. On Sunday, however, most ad-hungry editors refused to grant additional space to any strip, and only tabloid readers in general were able to enjoy full-length *Abners* and *Pogos* in full-panel size.

Gradually, as a result, realistic action and fine-art humor strips faded from the comic pages, and an increasing number of simplistically drawn he-said, she-said repartee-gag strips filled newspaper strip space. Some of these newcomers — *B.C.*, *The Wizard of Id*, *Peanuts* and others — were witty and wonderfully imaginative, building delightful new characters out of sheer graphic verve and a stunning sense of humor, but most were little better than space-fillers, driving still more readers from the comics. By the late 1960s, the newspaper comic strip had largely self-destructed as a measurably competent narrative art form, holding just a few sputtering Roman candles brightly aloft in an arena once fiery with inspired fireworks, but now dimly lit over its broad expanse only by inaudibly popping lady fingers and futilely fizzing sparklers.

A healthy number of well-handled strips emerged in the 1940s and later despite the growing problems of format and display, a good proportion pursuing the realistic crime, Western and science fiction genres which were hobbled in advance by the prevailing size restraints. The best of these, although severely crippled as visual narrative in their daily format, often managed to have some effective reader impact on the Sunday page, particularly where their syndicate distributors were able to persuade subscribing papers to give them an increasingly rare half-page layout. (At least four such strips made a valiant effort to obtain and hold full-page display space in a few papers, notably Warren Tufts' Civil War strip *Lance*, but slow reader response led to their fairly swift demise.)

The Western story theme was most strongly developed in Fred Harman's popular *Red Ryder* (a successor to the same artist's *Bronc Peeler*), which had the good fortune to have been launched in full-page format in many papers in 1940, building a readership which stayed loyal to the feature after its reduction to half-page, then third-page format, keeping it in print well into the 1950s. Warren Tufts' first Western, the brutally realistic and gripping half-page *Casey Ruggles*, ran a number of years in the 1950s, as did the beautifully drawn daily *The Cisco Kid* (which had an effective display in a few Hearst papers which tried to sustain pre-war daily strip size against the general newspaper tide). A few years later, the enormous success of old 1930s Westerns on TV led to a dumping of hastily contrived comic strip adaptations into the nation's strip sections built around the film work of "Hopalong Cassidy," Roy Rogers, Gene Autry and others, about which the less said the better.

In the crime action genre, a number of low-quality entries crowded the strip docket in the immediate wartime and post-war decades, but one or two, such as *Kerry Drake*, *Rip Kirby* and *Steve Roper* (a continuation of the pre-war *Big Chief Wahoo*), were marked by strong and effective strip narration. Later, a strip version of Mickey Spillane's *Mike Hammer* proved to be a genuinely gutsy reflection of the long-lasting novel series, and way too tough for the majority of newspapers.

In a genre all their own, the post-war military adventure strip, Milton Caniff and Roy Crane abandoned their classic pre-war work in *Terry and the Pirates* and *Captain Easy* to pursue Air Force and Navy interests, often in the guise of private adventurings, in Caniff's *Steve Canyon* and Crane's *Buz Sawyer* (while Crane's earlier strip was continued very effectively by his previous aide, Leslie Turner, and Caniff's much less so by a newcomer named George Wunder, who wasn't).

Science fiction was very well served in the post-war years by such outstanding strips as *Space Cadet*, *Twin Earths*, the time-travel sequences of *Alley Oop*, *Beyond Mars*, a fine continuing *Buck Rogers*, a new daily *Flash Gordon*, *Chris Welkin, Planeteer*, and others, to be eventually strangled by the same space limitations that brought all serious continuity strips to their finish or a lingering impotence.

Apart from a handful of dismal talking-head soaps, such as *Mary Worth* and *Apartment 3-G*, the rest of the post-war strip additions lay in the amorphous world of comedy. *Pogo* was the leader here, with *Krazy Kat* in its final years, followed by the quietly understated fantasy of *Barnaby and Mr. O'Malley*; the rollicking Mexican fiesta of *Gordo*, with its continual bursting of fresh *piñatas* of art and comedy; the dogged ill fortune of *The Sad Sack*, a wartime GI favorite which made a good comic-page impact well into the 1950s; *Archie*, a brilliantly funny strip adaptation of the famous comic book series; *Texas Slim and Dirty Dalton*, a highly successful post-war adaptation — incredibly — of a 1920s strip by its originator, Ferd Johnson; the deservedly world-famed *Peanuts*; the shy, wry, sweet *King Aroo*; the serio-comic *Brenda Starr* and its sister in funny suspense, *Invisible Scarlet O'Neil* (which later segued into the ultra-bizarre *Stainless Steel*); *The Sad Sack*'s sterling successor, *Beetle Bailey*, a monument to sustained character comedy; the bitter and sweet of family life memorably invoked in *Hi and Lois*; the absurdist slapstick of *Nancy*; the cookie-cutter graphic precision that sustained the visual impact of *Dennis the Menace*; the half-comic, half-grim Western realism of Stan Lynde's *Rick O'Shay* (whose devoted following was sustained for its successor, the wholly realistic thriller *Latigo*); *Long Sam*, an Al Capp-scripted strip featuring a female equivalent of his *Li'l Abner*; *Abie 'n' Slats*, another Capp-written comedy about a small-town boxer and his bizarre relatives, nicely drawn by Raeburn van Buren; *Gasoline Alley*, masterfully continued by first Dick Moores and then Jim Scancarelli; *Robin Malone*, a fantastic comedy about a go-getting businesswoman intercut with stunning graphic work by Bob Lubbers; *Hoosegow Herman*, a wartime strip about a beleaguered GI carried over into the 1940s by World War I's leading cartoonist, Wally Walgren; Ferd Johnson's gentle, graphically superb continuation of the old *Moon Mullins* strip; the ramshackle fancy of the comics' only witch strip,

Broom Hilda; and a fair number of other worthwhile works spread over the 1940–1980 years.

In the striking comic strip renaissance of the past decade and a half, a new sophisticated audience has been drawn to newspaper strips by the emergence of major new works — such nervy, imaginative, outspoken strips as *Doonesbury, Calvin and Hobbes, Zippy the Pinhead, Bloom County* and its successor *Outland, The Far Side* (not a strip, of course, but thematically linked in a quasi-panel strip manner); *Ernie, Mother Goose and Grimm, Luann, Ziggy, Cathy, For Better or Worse, Shoe,* and a score more. Since these are widely available in contemporary papers, we have only touched on these current works here, including a few typical episodes, and one supremely funny *Ernie* sequence.

These introductory remarks to the four chronological divisions of *The Comic Strip Century* were written for the sole purpose of keeping the reader aware of the remarkable developments in content and format the newspaper comic strip has gone through from 1896 to the present; there has been no attempt to approach the perimeters of critical history. The chief purpose of this book is to present as many examples of key comic strip episodes and stories from the past hundred years as possible, holding textual commentary to a minimum throughout.

As extensive and impressive as this collection is, it remains, of course, only the decorated antechamber of the century's newsprint palace of the comic strip (and of the pictorial narratives that preceded it); despite the two hundred volumes or more that have been published over the past decade, dozens upon dozens of important and memorable strips remain uncollected, unreprinted, and largely unread by contemporary eyes. The academics haven't done much here yet aside from looking into the reprinted collections — the reading load is too heavy and the academic rewards too meager in a book-oriented university world — so the fun and games of exploring the comic strip palace are still mostly yours.

The gates to the palace stand wide open, in every major library in the country, to be entered through their microfilm reader screens; via all of the actual newsprint pages held at the world's only definitive reference collection of the printed newspaper comic strip, the San Francisco Academy of Comic Art; or those remaining in bound newspaper volumes at the Boston Public Library (limited to Boston papers), the Library of Congress (limited to Washington, D.C., and Baltimore papers), the Madison State Historical Society (no Sunday comics), and perhaps a few other locations. Check out your local sources; you never know what you might find!

1895–1919

A SECRET SOCIETY INITIATION IN HOGAN'S ALLEY.

THE WORLD: SUNDAY, SEPTEMBER 20, 1896.—COMIC WEEKLY.

Made It a Coincidence.

"Look here!" he began as he entered the corner drug store at 10 o'clock in the evening. "I am tired of this sort of thing and propose to end it!"

"You refer to life?" queried the clerk as he moved towards the soda fountain.

"I do, sir! Under present circumstances it is not worth the living. Let it end right here and now! You have poisons?"

"Oh, of course—a large, fresh stock."

"Arsenic, strychnine and so forth?"

"Yes."

"If it wasn't for my wife I'd live on," said the caller as he picked up a bottle of Florida water and sniffed at the end of it. "She'd drive a saint to his grave."

"I see."

"When she sees my dead face she may regret her line of conduct. I tell you, it's an awful thing to drive a good man to suicide."

"What syrup will you take?" queried the clerk as he rinsed a glass.

"Syrup? I want poison! No one asked you for soda-water."

"I know; but you see your wife was in here half an hour ago. She said she was also tired of life."

"She did, eh? Sure it was my wife?"

"Oh, yes. She also wanted poison to end her career. Said if it wasn't for you she'd try and live on, but you were such a mean cuss that she'd rather die."

"And my wife said that!" persisted the other.

"Every word of it, sir; and I didn't know, but you might want to make a curious coincidence of it."

"How—how do you mean?"

"Why, she finally decided to take sarsaparilla soda and live on for a few days. Shall we say sarsaparilla and curious coincidence?"

"Well, you know"—

"But under the circumstances?"

"Well, then, under the circumstances I'll take the same as she did and live on, but she must look upon this as a great moral warning—a great moral warning, sir! Yes—sarsaparilla and plenty of water in it!"

He'd Done His Duty.

He had done his duty.

He smiled with conscious pride. His chest puffed out, and he trod the earth with elate footsteps.

His very air convinced those around him that no dipterous insects could find any lodgment on his person.

He had done his duty.

A glow irridated his countenance, and at times he laughed aloud.

Twice or thrice he roared with jollity.

He had done his duty, and was proud of it.

"Say," he said to some of his acquaintances who had met him at the steamer landing, as they repaired to a nearby saloon, "them Custom-House inspectors is blind as beetles! Did I do 'em? Well, watch me!"

Unbuttoning his vest he disclosed several layers of silks. From his pocket he extracted about half a dozen diamonds of the first water, and he passed around samples of some cigars of which, he said, he had a thousand more at the bottom of his trunks.

He had done his duty with a vengeance.

WHAT THEY DID TO THE DOG-CATCHER IN HOGAN'S ALLEY.

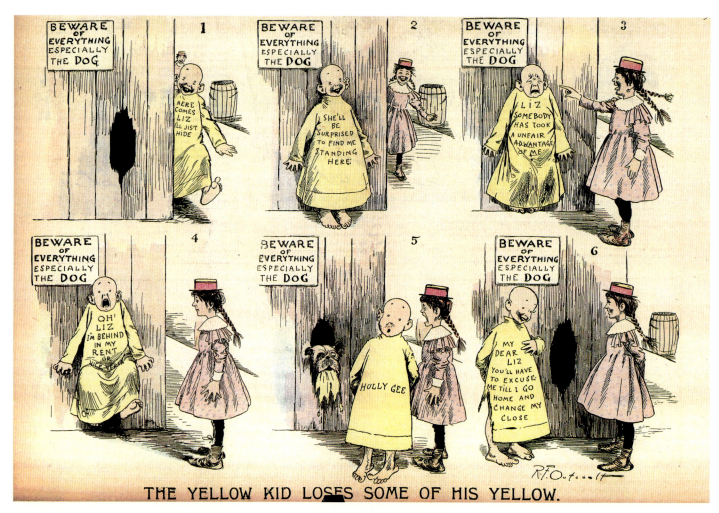

1897

THE KATZENJAMMER KIDS 1898 RUDOLPH DIRKS

1902

The Katzenjammer Kids Explore a Ship.

HANS UND FRITZ
EX-PIRATE JOHN
by RUDOLPH DIRKS, Originator of the Katzenjammer Kids

THE CAPTAIN AND THE KIDS

By R. Dirks, Originator of the Katzenjammer Kids

HUGO HERCULES · 1902 · J. KOERNER

HUGO HERCULES MISSES THE FOOTBALL, BUT—

1903

When the Comic Supplement Arrives on Mt. Ararat.

Opening Night of the Opera "The Cherry Tree" on Mt. Ararat.

HOW LEANDER POPPED THE QUESTION

1. LEANDER (aside): "Confound it all! I'll NEVER get a chance to tell Lulu of my love. Her popper and mommer have kept right at our heels during the entire week. I feel like giving up."

2. LULU'S POPPER: "Oh, isn't the view delightful from here!" CHORUS: "G-l-o-r-i-o-u-s!"

3. LULU: "O-o-o-o-h! Popper and mommer have fallen over the precipice!" LEANDER: "Lulu—quick—now we are alone! I love you. Will you be my wife?"

4. LULU: "Yes, yes! Why didn't you ever ask me before? Certainly! But hurry, hurry! Save them! Save them!" LEANDER: "Hoop la! I could save the world now!"

5. LULU: "Saved! Saved! Saved!" LEANDER: "Hold on, we will be there soon!"

6. LULU'S POPPER: "You have saved our lives. A hero for a son-in-law! Hoop la!" LULU'S MOMMER: "I always did like Leander. So noble and brave. I'll make him just the loveliest mother-in-law."

ALPHONSE AND GASTON IN INDIA.
They and Their Friend Leon Have a Mix-up with the Idol Juggernaut.

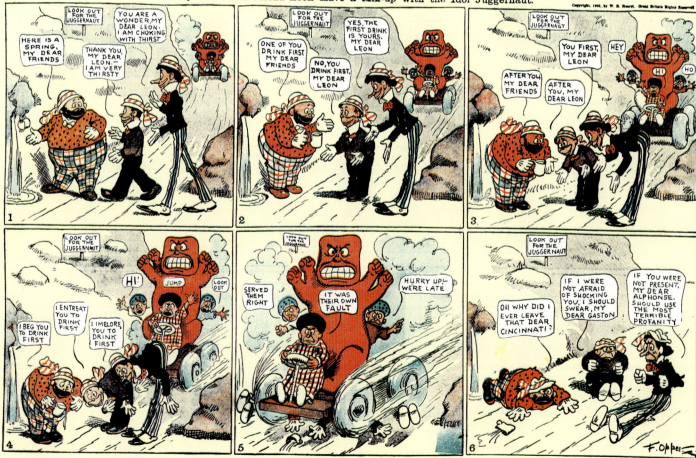

AN AUCTION SALE ON MT. ARARAT.

THE KATZENJAMMER KIDS GIVE A FEW IMITATIONS.

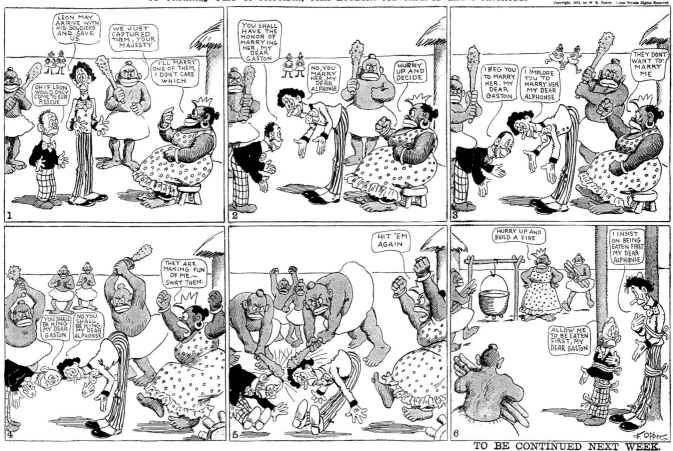

ALPHONSE, GASTON AND THEIR FRIEND LEON IN THE ARCTIC REGIONS.
A Story of Thrilling Adventures and Never-Failing Politenss. In Three Chapters. Chapter 2.
SYNOPSIS OF LAST SUNDAY'S INSTALLMENT: While hunting for rare birds Alphonse and Gaston fell over the cliff, and would have fallen several million miles if they hadn't caught hold of a branch.

Panel 1:
- Leon (top): "AH, MY POOR FRIENDS"
- Alphonse: "THIS BRANCH WILL NOT HOLD US BOTH. I WILL DROP AND YOU SHALL BE SAVED, MY DEAR GASTON"
- Gaston: "LET ME DROP, AND YOU SHALL BE SAVED, MY DEAR ALPHONSE"

Panel 2:
- Leon: "I SHALL MOURN YOU DEEPLY"
- Alphonse: "I INSIST ON DROPPING, IN ORDER TO SAVE YOUR LIFE, MY DEAR GASTON"
- Gaston: "I DEMAND TO DROP IN ORDER TO SAVE YOUR LIFE, MY DEAR ALPHONSE"

Panel 3:
- Leon: "HAVE YOU ANY LAST WORDS TO SAY, MY DEAR FRIENDS?"
- Alphonse: "I WILL SACRIFICE MYSELF, MY DEAR GASTON"
- Gaston: "NEVER!— I WILL SACRIFICE MYSELF, MY DEAR ALPHONSE"

Panel 4:
- Leon: "I WILL SEE THAT YOUR GRAVES ARE KEPT GREEN"
- Alphonse: "I SHALL BE IN DESPAIR IF YOU DO NOT LET ME SACRIFICE MY LIFE"
- Gaston: "I SHALL BE DESOLATED IF YOU DO NOT LET ME DROP"

Panel 5:
- Leon: "FAREWELL, MY DEAR FRIENDS. YOU SHALL HAVE A MAGNIFICENT FUNERAL"

(TO BE CONCLUDED NEXT SUNDAY.)

ALPHONSE, GASTON AND THEIR FRIEND LEON IN THE ARCTIC REGIONS.
A Story of Thrilling Adventures and Never-Failing Politenss. In Three Chapters. Chapter 3.
SYNOPSIS OF PREVIOUS INSTALLMENTS: Alphonse and Gaston fell from the top of the cliff.

Panel 1:
- Leon: "THANK GOODNESS THEY ARE NOT HURT"
- Alphonse: "I AM GLAD YOU ARE NOT HURT, MY DEAR GASTON"
- Gaston: "I AM DELIGHTED TO SEE THAT YOU ARE UNINJURED, MY DEAR ALPHONSE"

Panel 2:
- Leon: "I WILL CLIMB DOWN AND HELP THEM"
- Bear: "COME CHILDREN DINNER'S READY"
- Alphonse: "THERE IS A POLAR BEAR AND HER CUBS"
- Gaston: "FLY, MY DEAR ALPHONSE, AND I WILL STAY AND BE EATEN"

Panel 3:
- Leon: "I AM FALLING"
- Cubs: "WE'RE HUNGRY"
- Alphonse: "NO, I WILL STAY AND BE EATEN"
- Gaston: "I DEMAND TO STAY AND BE EATEN"

Panel 4: (Leon falls on the bears)

Panel 5:
- Bear: "LET'S GO HOME CHILDREN— I HAVE A TERRIBLE BACKACHE"
- Alphonse: "YOU ARE A HERO, MY DEAR LEON"
- Gaston: "YOU HAVE SAVED US, MY DEAR LEON"
- Leon: "DO NOT MENTION IT, MY DEAR FRIENDS"

F. Opper

1895–1919

THE BROWNIES IN THE PHILIPPINES   1903   PALMER COX

LEON BUYS A PARROT FOR THAT DEAR COUNTESS

Our Happy Family Celebrates the Glorious Fourth!

By the Sad Sea Waves!

THE DOINGS OF HAPPY HOOLIGAN AND HIS BROTHER, GLOOMY GUS.
How Happy Helped with the Flying Machine. A Thrilling Tale of Adventure in Two Chapters—Chapter 1.

THE DOINGS OF HAPPY HOOLIGAN AND HIS BROTHER, GLOOMY GUS.
How Happy Helped with the Flying Machine. A Thrilling Tale of Adventure and Hard Luck—(Concluded).
SYNOPSIS OF LAST WEEK'S INSTALLMENT—Happy Hooligan went up in a balloon, and the balloon exploded. Happy landed on his head in an automobile, upset the occupant and—here he is.

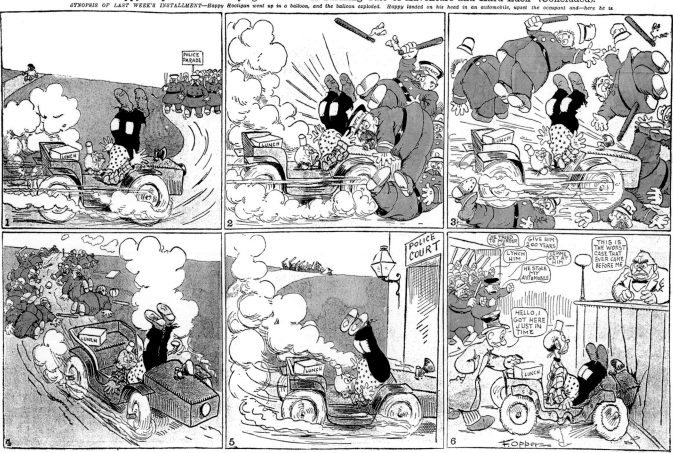

Poor Happy Hooligan! The Night Was Dark and Stormy!

AND HER NAME WAS MAUD!

(To be Continued Next Sunday)

1. "Naubau." said the Scarecrow.
2. Danced a graceful jig.
3. "Don't get frightened."
4. Fishes of many colors.
5. A Plant sprang into sight.

What was the name of the tree?

Dorothy Spends an Evening With Her Old Friends and is Entertained With Wonderful Exhibitions

DOROTHY had come to spend an evening with her old friends from Oz, who were occupying pleasant rooms provided for them by the Mayor of the city.

"It does seem like old times to be with folks from the Land of Oz again," said she. "I think the reason I love you all is because you are so different."

"Yes," remarked the Scarecrow, thoughtfully, "I have learned since we came to visit America that we are quite different from your earth people. They call us fairies, and think everything we do is the result of magic."

"But, really, you are fairies, in a way," declared little Dorothy, "and you do wonderful things."

"You people also do wonderful things," said the Wogglebug, who was present; "but no one here seems surprised at moving-pictures, talking-machines, or telephones—which surely owe their origin to magical arts."

"That is because we are used to them," the little girl replied. "The things that interest us are those we seldom see. Won't you perform some of your own magic for me this evening?"

"With great pleasure," answered the Scarecrow. "It is our duty to strive to amuse our guests, and we will attempt to do some things you seldom see in America."

As he spoke he looked around the room and noticed, hanging upon the wall, a full-length picture of an old gentleman standing in a gilt frame. Folding his arms behind his back the Scarecrow uttered the magic word: "Naubau!"

At once the old gentleman stepped from the background of the picture and made a polite bow to the company. Then he unfastened the empty frame from the wall, caught it under his left arm, and began to dance a graceful and dignified jig, while the Wogglebug whistled a tune for accompaniment.

Dorothy watched him with great delight, and when he had completed his dance the old gentleman wiped his brow with his handkerchief, made another bow, hung the gilt frame upon its nail, and then stepped back into it. Next moment he was a picture again, flat and motionless as before.

"That was very interesting," said Dorothy.

The Tin Woodman now stepped forward and made three magic signs, one after the other.

"Look out," said he; "but don't get frightened."

Then he took off his funnel-shaped hat and held it in front of him, and immediately a stream of water rushed from the funnel and fell upon the carpet. Dorothy screamed a little and stood upon her chair to keep from getting wet.

Faster and faster came the water from the funnel, flooding all the floor of the room, and rising steadily until it almost reached the seats of the chairs on which all the party were now perched.

The Tin Woodman spoke a queer word that sounded like "chugaremohmchug!" and at once the little girl perceived enormous fishes swimming in the water. They were of many brilliant colors and all were lighted from within themselves, so that their bright colored scales glowed like the stained-glass windows of churches.

While the girl looked on wonderingly the Tin Woodman spoke another word and replaced the funnel upon his head. At once the gorgeous fish disappeared; the flood subsided, and—strange to say—not a drop of moisture remained upon the carpet or furniture to show where the water had been.

"That was strange and beautiful!" said Dorothy, with a sigh, as she resumed her seat upon the chair.

It was now the Wogglebug's turn. The wise insect took a flower-pot filled with fresh earth and proceeded to bury a seed within the soil. Then he set the flower-pot upon the floor and said:

"Usually, as you know, it takes many years for a tree to grow from a seed. That is because Nature supplies very slowly the elements of chemistry required to enable the tree to increase in size, and therefore is obliged to grow just as slowly. But to-night I shall give the seed a large quantity of the food it requires to make it grow, and you will be surprised at the result."

He now crossed two fingers of his right upper hand, three fingers of his left upper hand, and four fingers of his right lower hand. Then with his left lower hand he made rapid circles above the flower-pot. At once a plant sprang into sight, rising higher and higher and spreading its breadth until it reached the ceiling, while its many branches nearly filled the room. Birds then appeared upon the limbs of this magic tree, warbling sweet songs; and although the night without was cold and dreary, this beautiful tree seemed to breathe a fragrance of summer and sunshine.

Dorothy's eyes were fixed admiringly upon the tree when the Wogglebug made a quick movement with all his four arms—a signal well known in magic by the people of Oz.

At once the tree shrank down into the pot and disappeared, and the room resumed its former appearance.

"That was indeed wonderful!" exclaimed the little girl. "What kind of a tree was it that you made to grow?"

"I'll tell you," said the Wogglebug, and he whispered to her the name of the tree.

L. FRANK BAUM.

What Did the Wogglebug Say? It's Worth Money to Know. See News Section.

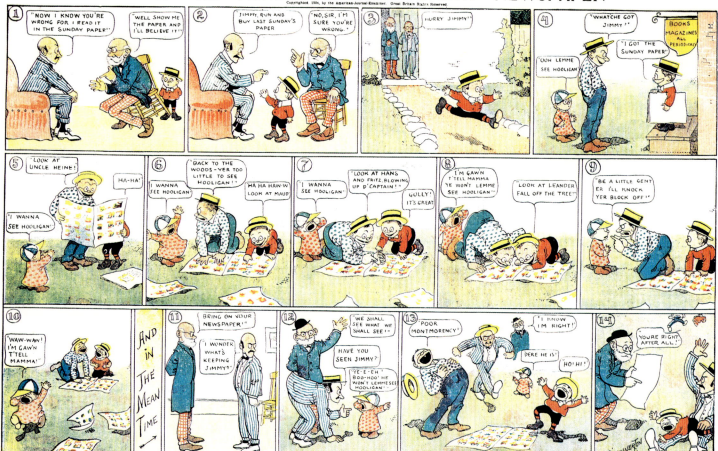

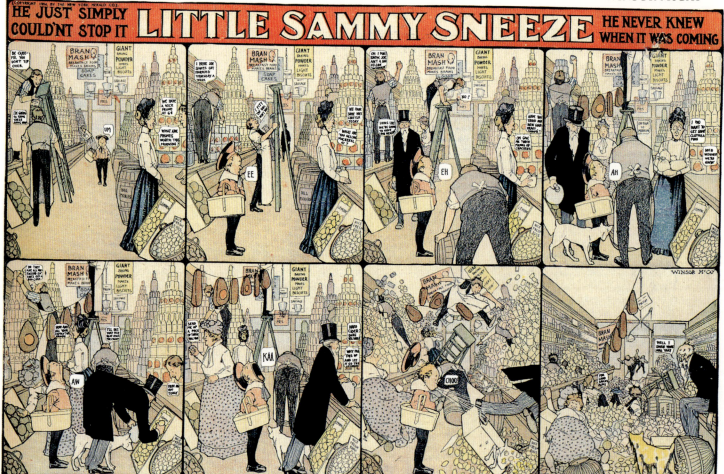

HUNGRY HENRIETTA — 1905 — WINSOR McCAY

DREAM OF THE RAREBIT FIEND — 1906 — WINSOR McCAY

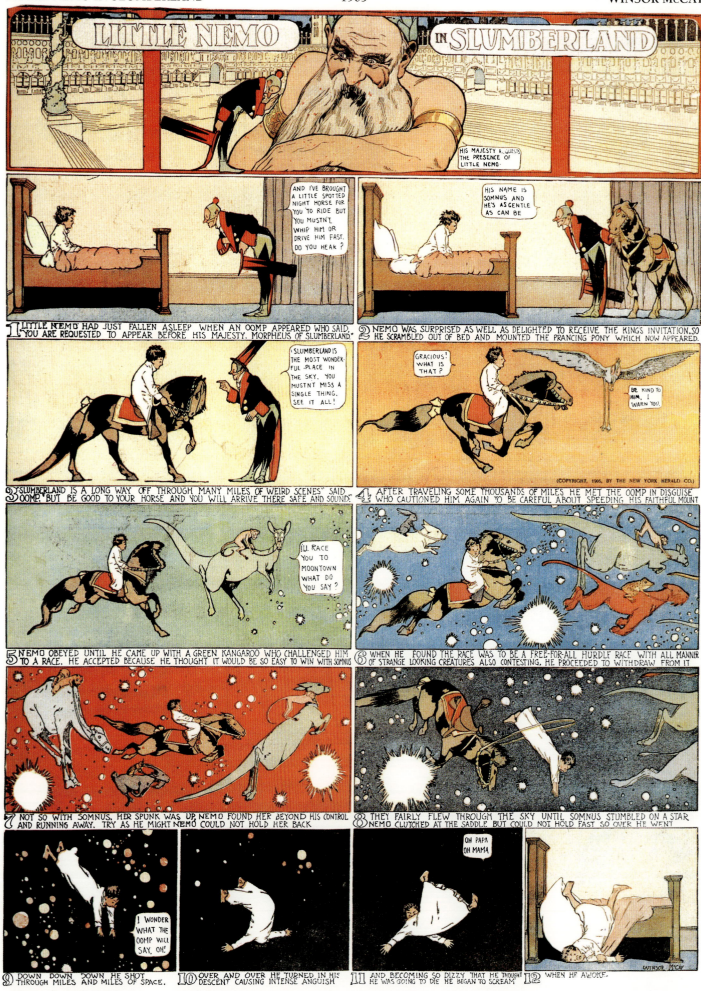

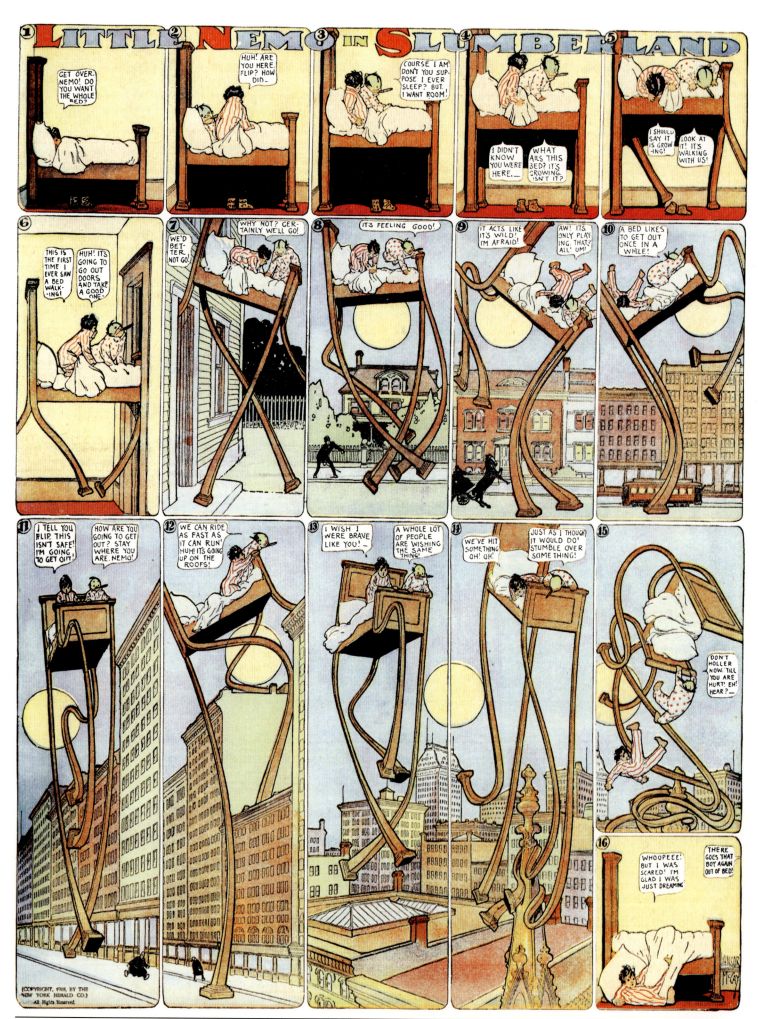

THE UPSIDE DOWNS — 1904 — GUSTAVE VERBECK

UPSIDE-DOWNS OF LITTLE LADY LOVEKINS AND OLD MAN MUFFAROO
THE BOY and the BEAN-STALK

(COPYRIGHT, 1904, BY THE NEW YORK HERALD CO.)

It has been raining, but now it has stopped, and little Lady Lovekins and Old Man Muffaroo can shut their umbrellas.

"I wonder what adventure we will meet with to-day!" says Lovekins. Presently they perceive a boy who seems to be very much alarmed at their approach.

The boy wears a black jockey cap. He throws himself on the ground, and pulling a small bean out of his pocket he plants it. Instantly it takes root and sprouts up.

"Good-bye," says the boy jumping at the top of the rapidly growing plant. About a mile a minute it grows, and the boy is very soon lost to sight in the clouds.

"This is marvelous!" cries Old Man Muffaroo. "Oh, let us climb up this bean-stalk," says Lovekins, "and we will see what there is at the top."

So they go up, and when Muffaroo gets tired of carrying the umbrellas he hands them to Lovekins,

THE WOOZLEBEASTS — 1904

The Gant, which is forced to eat lime
Has a courage that's simply sublime.
You'll admit it's no dream—you can see by the steam
He is having the deuce of a time.

When the tramp, waking up from his slumber,
Found himself face to face with the Bumba
He observed, "You old scamp" (he was nervy, the tramp)
"I will do you up yet, you back number."

"I will taste," said the Trink, "one or two
Just to see if the warning is true."
At the inquest they said it was Indian red
Mixed with too much cerulean blue.

The short, chunky, sunny faced Bille
Often beats his competitors till
The foot of the slope, when he gives up all hope,
For he makes all his speed down the hill.

When the vessels that pass in the night
See the weird old Bazeen with his light
Then the sailormen know it is going to snow
And they button their overcoats tight.

"I suppose I am getting on fine
Said the Jank as he hauled at the line.
"But using a winch for amusement's no cinch—
In vacation, small weakfish for mine"

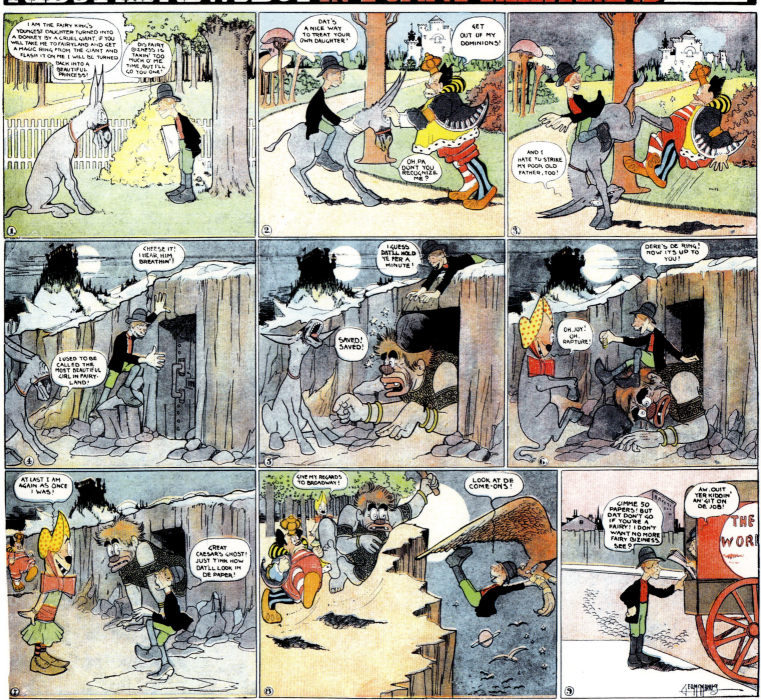

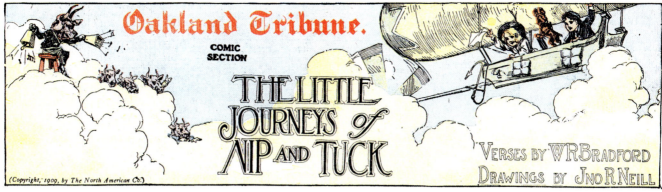

THE FINEHEIMER TWINS　　　　　　　　1909　　　　　　　　HAROLD KNERR

THE ADVENTURES OF MR. GEORGE　　　　　　　　1910　　　　　　　　HAROLD KNERR

OLD OPIE DILLDOCK'S STORIES

THE LITTLE POSSUM GANG. FIAH! FIAH!

THE LITTLE POSSUM GANG. CALLED THE WRONG ARMY

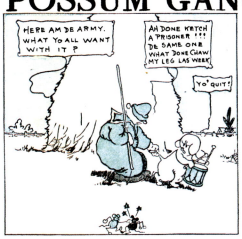

THE FAMILY UPSTAIRS

1911

GEORGE HERRIMAN

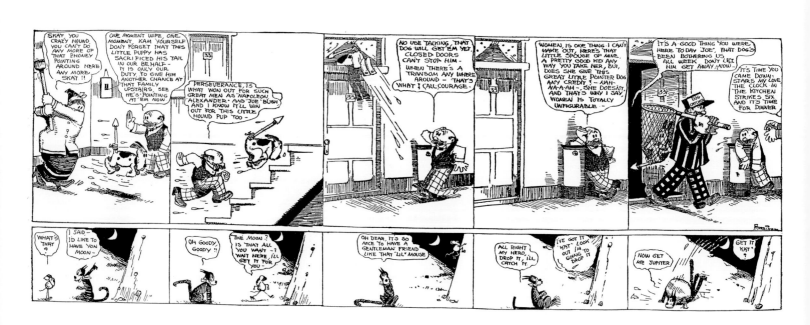

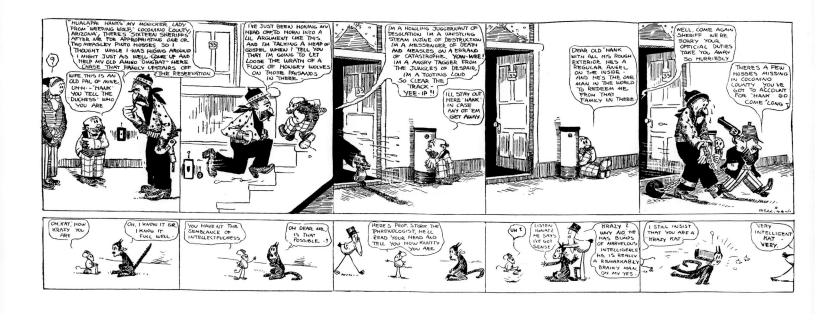

MR. TWEE DEEDLE

1—One day Dickie and Mr. Twee Deedle were walking down the street, when they saw a poor, aged man reaching for an apple when the owner of the fruit stand was not looking.

2—Dickie and Mr. Twee Deedle stepped up to him and said, "Oh, Mister, it's wrong to steal things!"

3—"I know it is," the aged man answered, as his eyes filled with tears. "But my sister has wished for an apple and I could not make the money to pay for it, so I thought perhaps the man would not miss just one apple!"

4—Mr. Twee Deedle asked him where he lived, and the man, asking them to follow, led them up many flights of stairs to where his sister was waiting for him.

The aged man told Mr. Twee Deedle and Dickie that he was a violinist and that he had come to the city many years ago to make his living playing, but since he had grown old he could not play so well and had to play at street corners to keep the two from starving.

6—Mr. Twee Deedle felt sorry for the brother and sister, and he and Dickie caught hold of the two and flew up over the buildings and—

7—Away out to the country, where the trees were green and there would be no one to disturb them. "For," said Mr. Twee Deedle, "we wish to hear you play the violin as you used to play it, so I will make both of you young again."

8—The brother and sister were delighted to be young again and thanked Mr. Twee Deedle.

9—Then the brother began playing a very beautiful piece. The little sprites and fairies, hearing the music, came flying to the spot, and all joined in a dance through the air, which they called the fairy ring. So when you are walking through the woods and think you hear soft music you may be sure that you hear the brother playing for the fairies and his sister to dance.

Laugh and the World Laughs With You

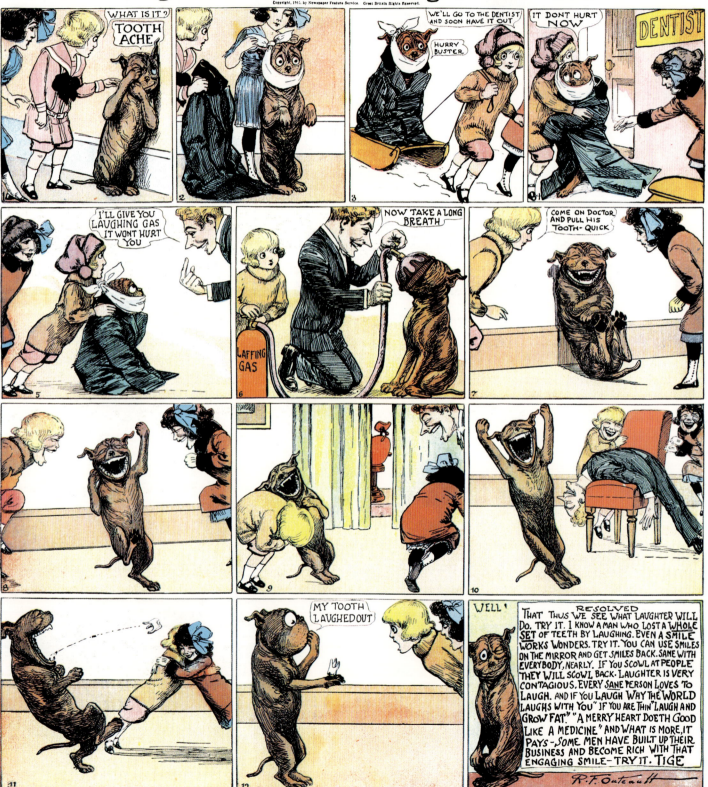

Krazy Kat By Herriman

1895–1919

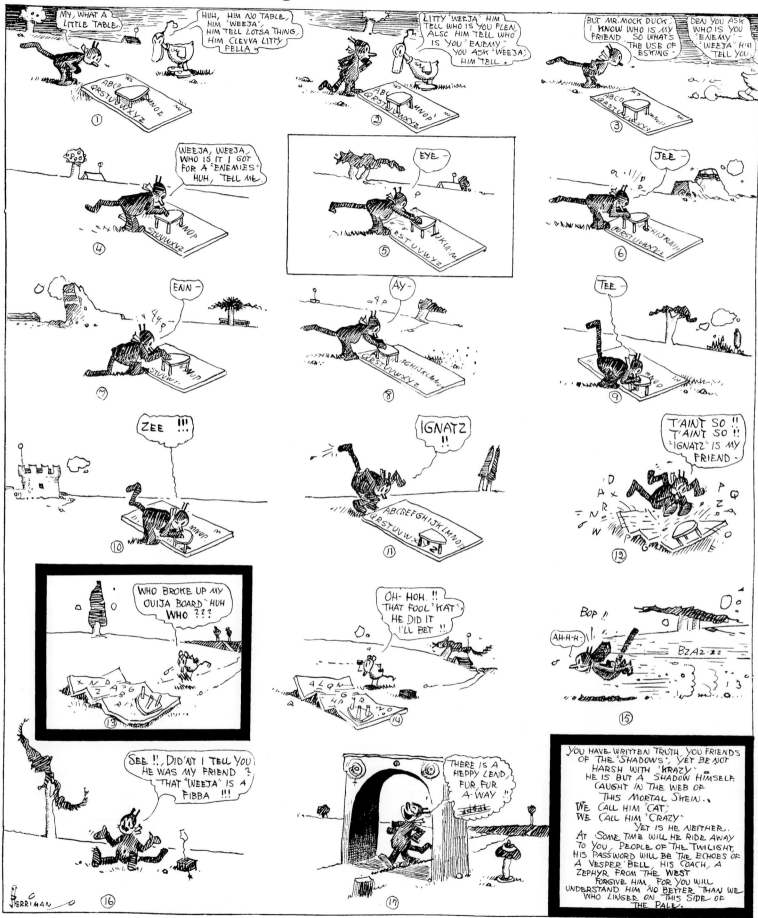

Krazy Kat — By Herriman

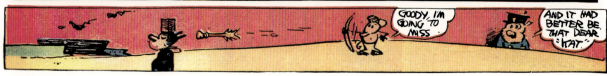

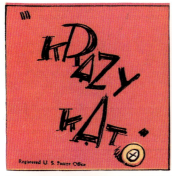

MUTT AND JEFF :·: A Merry Christmas—But Not for Jeff :·: By BUD FISHER

NOW LISTEN MABEL

1919 — GEORGE HERRIMAN

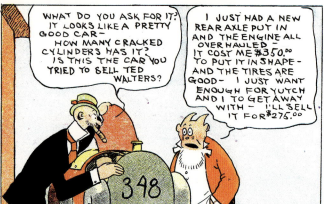
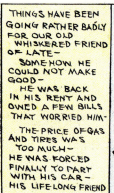

1920–1929

Bringing Up Father

Bringing Up Father

Bringing Up Father

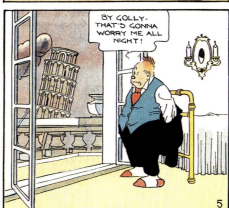

Jerry on the Job

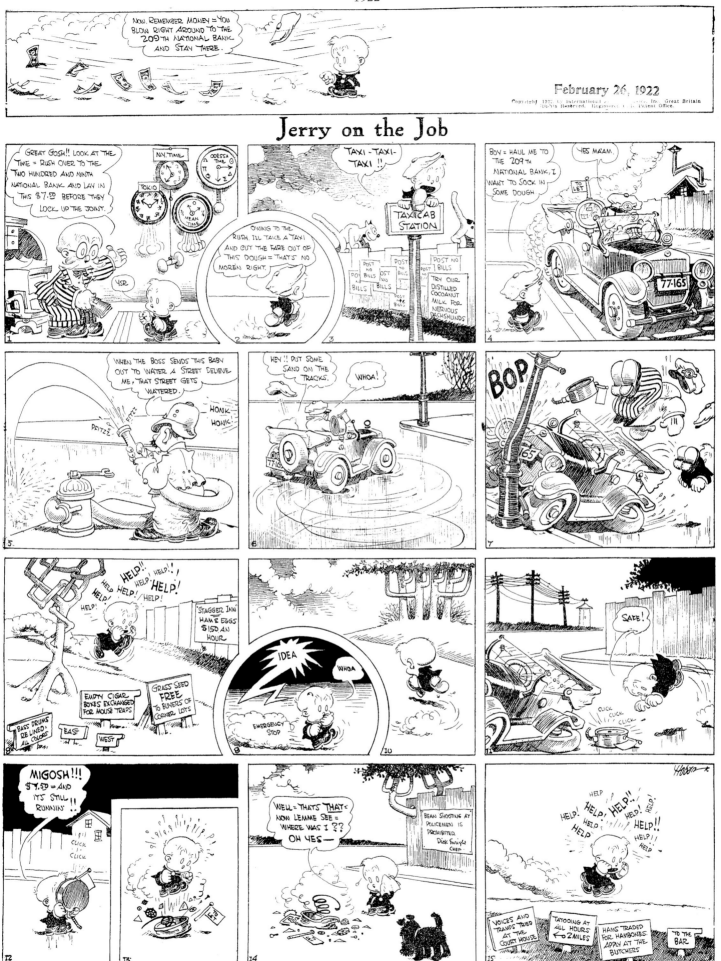

Just Boy—Poor "Gyp"! But It May Be More Like "Poor Pa"

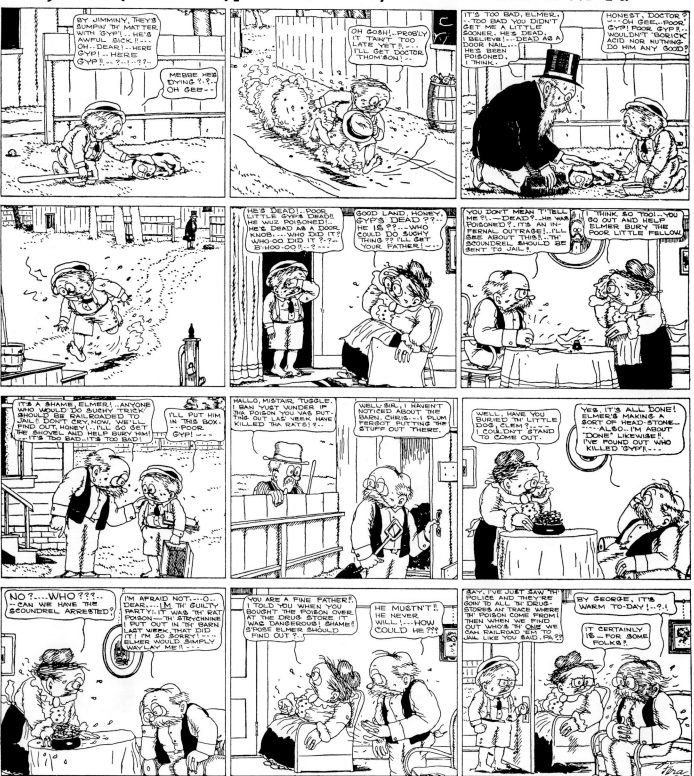

STUMBLE INN — 1922 — GEORGE HERRIMAN

THE GUMPS 1923 SIDNEY SMITH

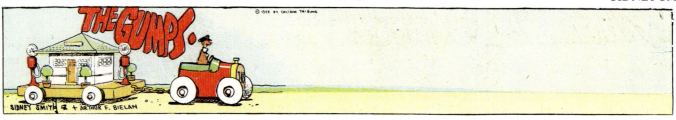

The Gumps — 1925 — Sidney Smith

Barney Google and Spark Plug

Barney Google and Spark Plug

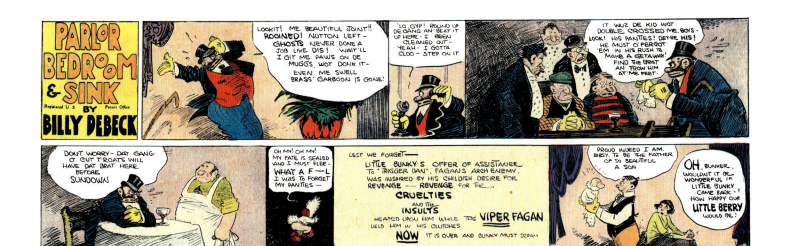

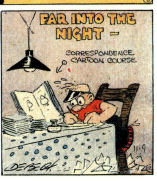

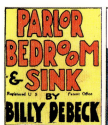

Barney Google and Spark Plug

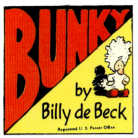

Barney Google

Barney Google — 1929 — Billy De Beck

Little Jimmy

Barney Google and Spark Plug

Tillie the Toiler

Boob McNutt

1920–1929

Happy Hooligan

Toots and Casper

The Katzenjammer Kids

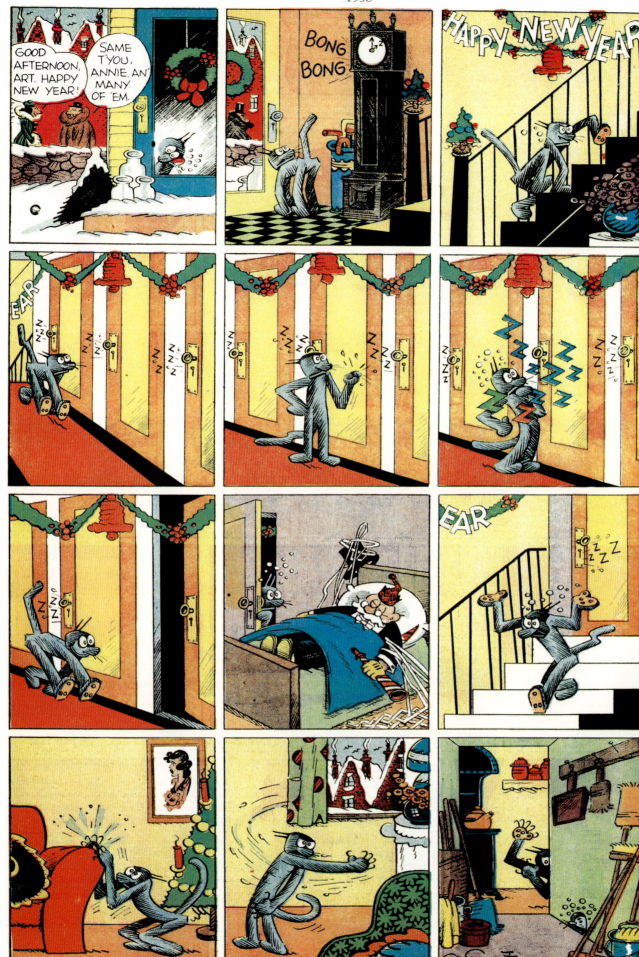

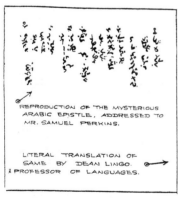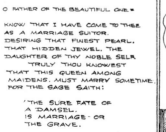

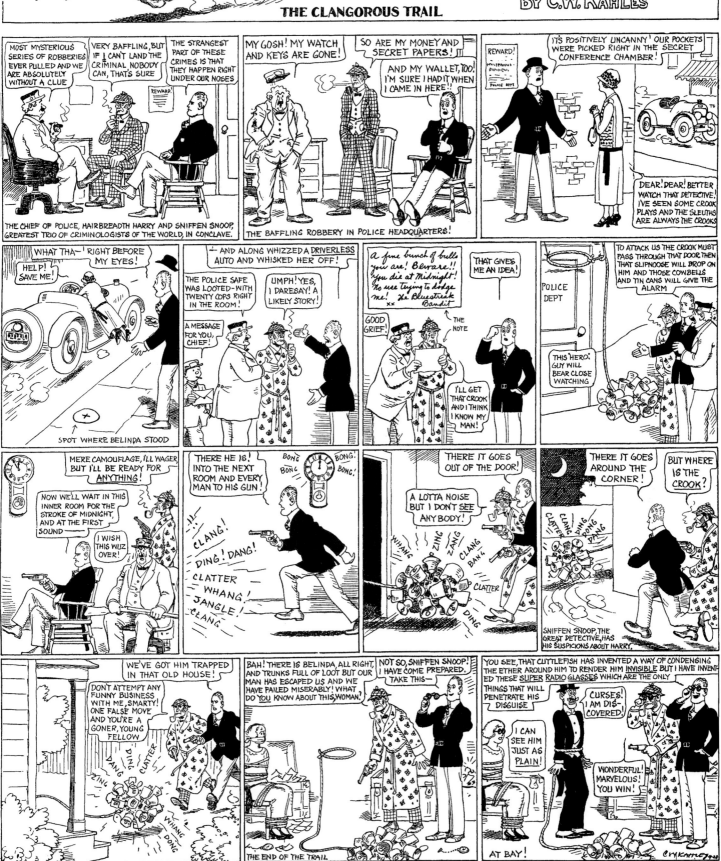

SALESMAN SAM — 1924 — GEORGE SWAN

The Katzenjammer Kids

  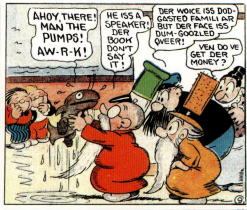
  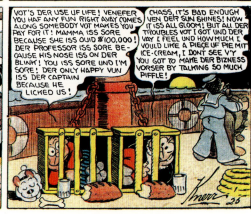

The Katzenjammer Kids

  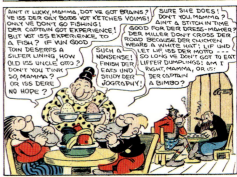

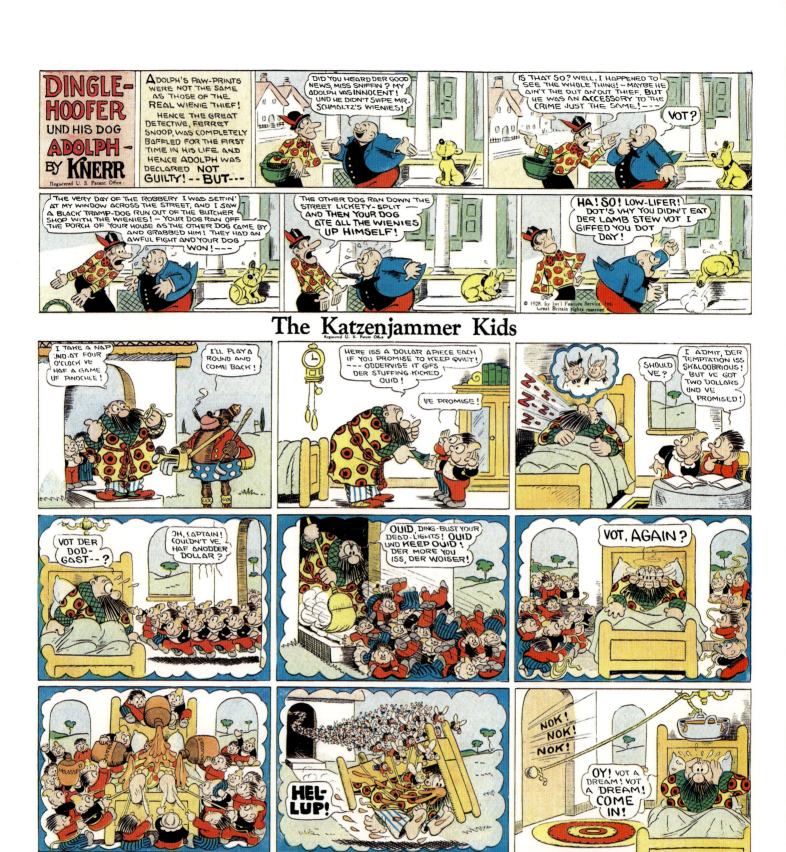
The Katzenjammer Kids

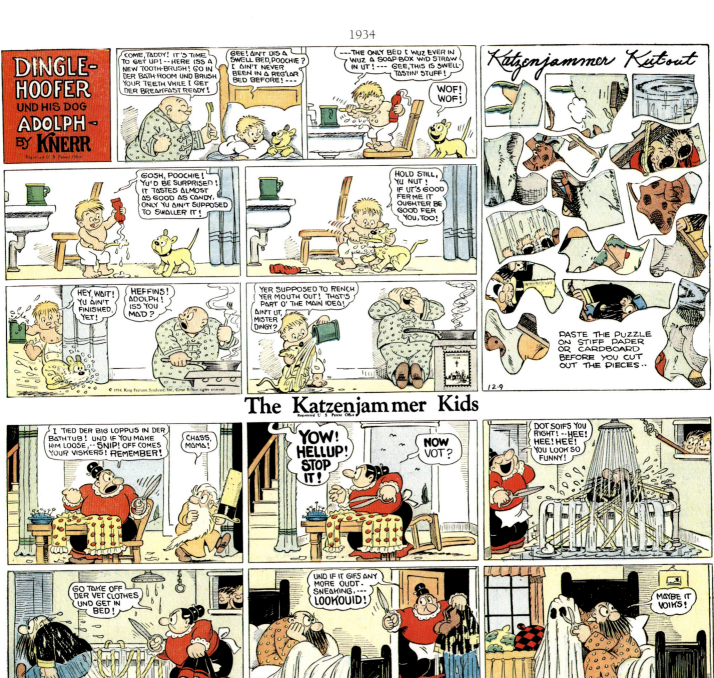

TOONERVILLE FOLKS   The Skipper's Brain Isn't Wooden Anyhow   By Fontine Fox

GASOLINE ALLEY — 1925 — FRANK KING

THRILLING ADVENTURES OF COUNT BRIC A BRAC — 1926 — LUDWIG BEMELMANS

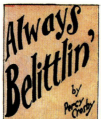

Skippy

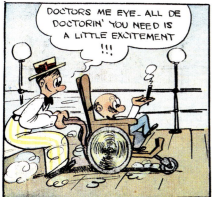

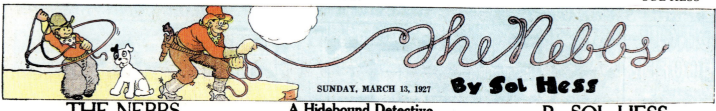

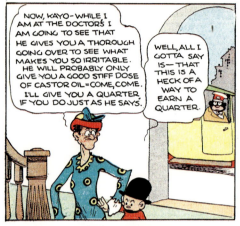

Moon Mullins — 1926 — Fred Willard

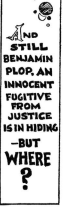

1920–1929

THIMBLE THEATRE — 1928 — E. C. SEGAR

EMBARRASSING MOMENTS — 1929 — GEORGE HERRIMAN

SCHOOL DAYS

Every Day in Every Way the Monkey-Wrench
Is Becoming Mightier Than the Sword.

By Dwig

COUNT SCREWLOOSE OF TOOLOOSE

By Milt Gross

Dave's Delicatessen

1930–1939

BOOB McNUTT — 1930 — RUBE GOLDBERG

Boob McNutt

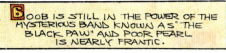

Boob McNutt

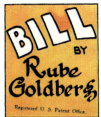

Boob McNutt

Felix

Thimble Theatre

Thimble Theatre

Thimble Theatre

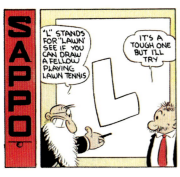

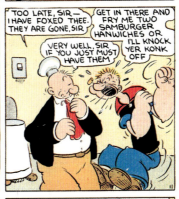

JOE PALOOKA — 1930 — HAM FISHER

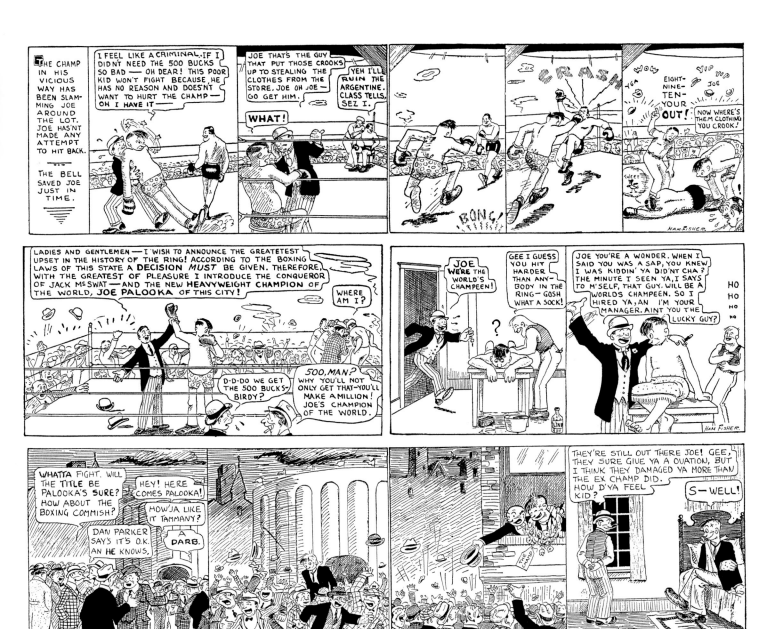

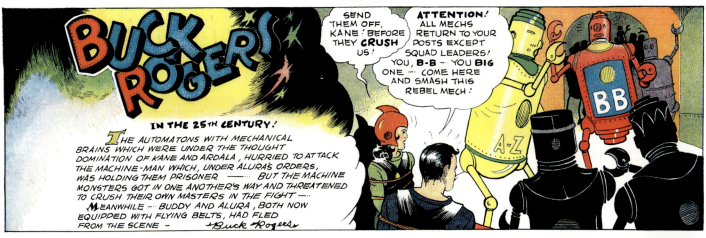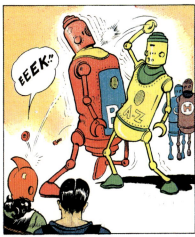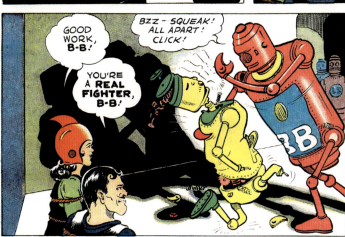

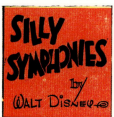

Mickey Mouse

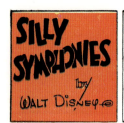

Mickey Mouse

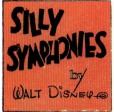   

Mickey Mouse

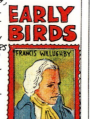

CITY SHADOWS — by Percy Crosby

PERCY CROSBY
The Distinguished Creator of "Skippy"

"Janitor, will you tell me if the sun is shining? I want to take the baby out."

Childhood Tragedies — by Percy Crosby
The Distinguished Creator of "Skippy"

"Dear Lord, please make Mama an' Papa stop fightin' 'cause it's hard to take sides when you love them both, an' besides, I'm ashamed to face the kids."

Just-Kids

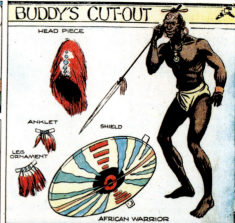

Tim Tyler's Luck

···Nothin' But A Hoss···

I knew him when he first was foaled—
He was pretty close to nine years old.
No use in me a feelin' blue.,
There was nothin' else fer me to do—
— And — HE'S NOTHIN' BUT A HOSS······

Seems a pity to me though—,
That this is how he had to go.
He sure could haze th' orneriest cow;
Confound me! What's th' matter now?
— HE'S NOTHIN' BUT A HOSS ·········

His mouth was tough—so was his hide—
An' he gave me many a hard old ride.
He had me, an' I had him—
On ranges fair or fat, or slim;
Shucks — HE'S NOTHIN' BUT A HOSS····

Them danged brown eyes was full o' pain.
I stroked his nose an' pulled his mane.
Heck! HE'S NOTHIN' BUT A HOSS······

He knew his time had come to die;
So he looked me bravely in the eye.
Heck! HE'S NOTHIN' BUT A HOSS·····

He's just hair an' meat an' bone,
But I hate to leave him there alone.
I think I'll swear — NAW! I don't cry
That doggone sand got in my eye.
BESIDES — HE'S NOTHIN' BUT A HOSS.

POEM WRITTEN BY RAY HARRIS.

THE COMIC STRIP CENTURY

THE COMIC STRIP CENTURY

CELEBRATING 100 YEARS OF AN AMERICAN ART FORM

EDITED BY BILL BLACKBEARD AND DALE CRAIN

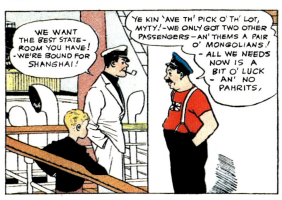
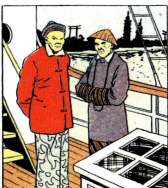

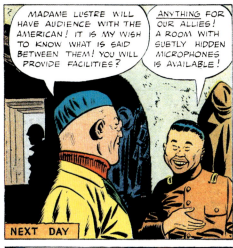

1942

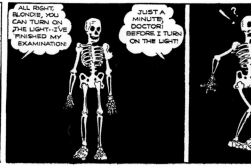

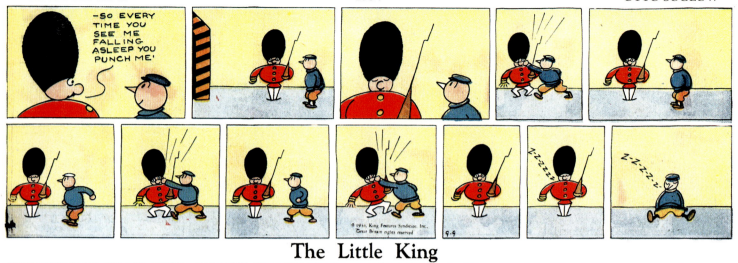

The Little King

SECRET AGENT X-9 1934 DASHIELL HAMMETT • ALEX RAYMOND

THE ADVENTURES OF PATSY — 1934 — MEL GRAFF

OUT OUR WAY — 1934 — J. R. WILLIAMS

OUR BOARDING HOUSE — 1934 — GENE AHERN

SCORCHY SMITH — 1935 — NOEL SICKLES

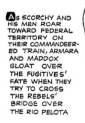

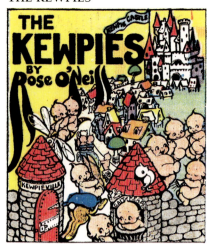

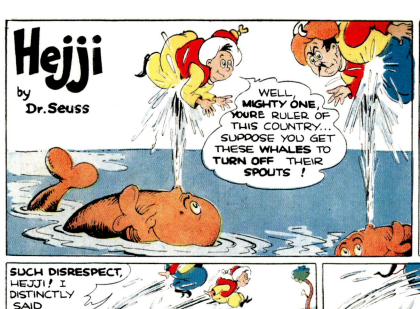

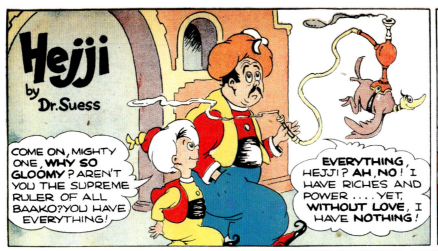

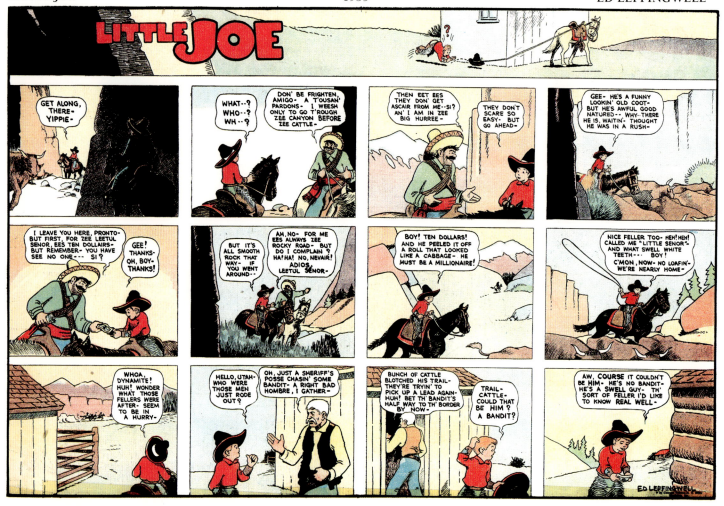

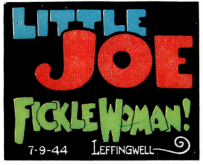

SMILIN' JACK — 1935 — ZACK MOSLEY

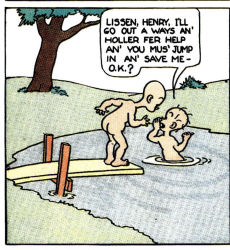

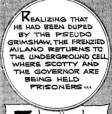

THE BUNGLE FAMILY — 1935 — HARRY J. TUTHILL

1930–1939

1930–1939

MINUTE MOVIES — 1935 — ED WHEELAN

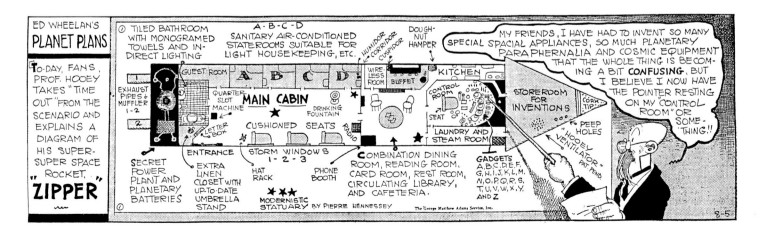

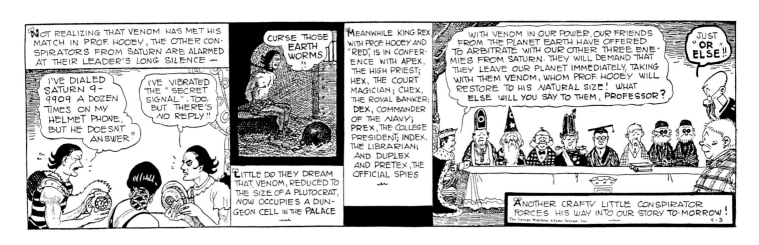

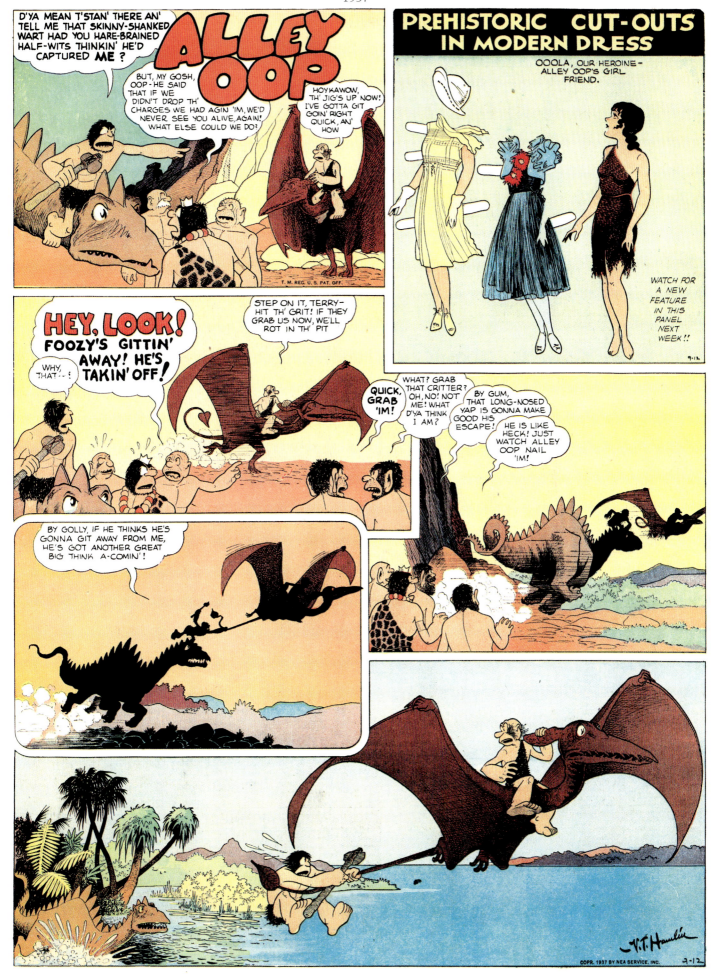

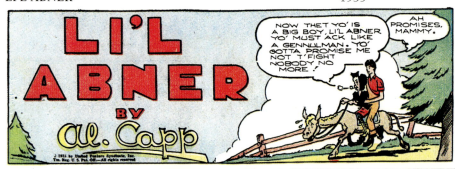

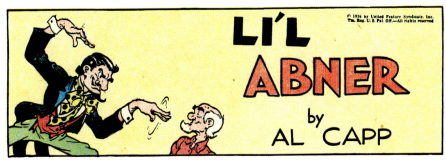

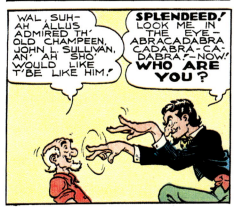

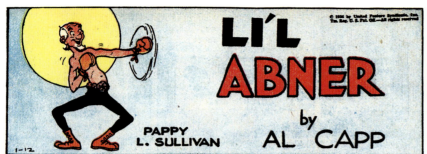

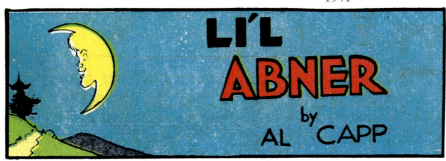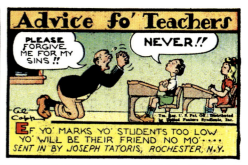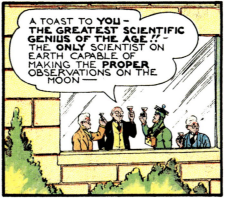

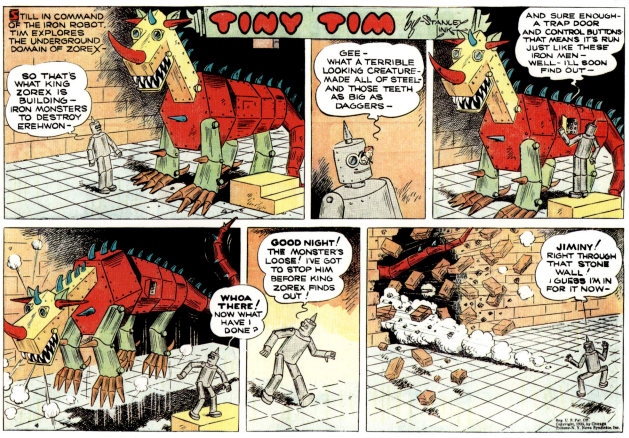
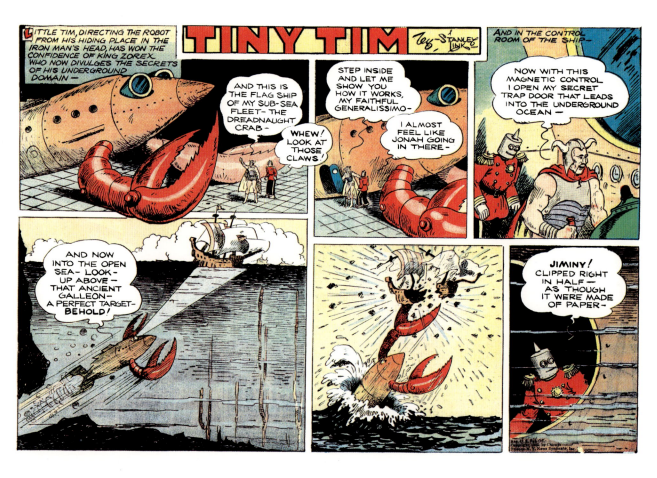

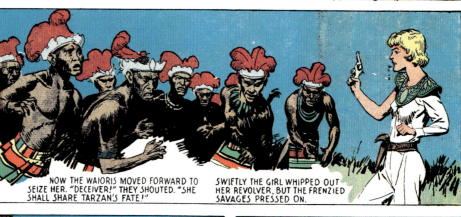

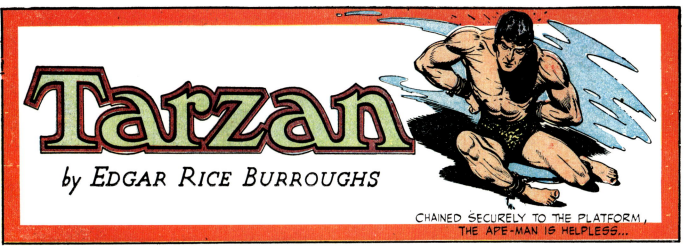

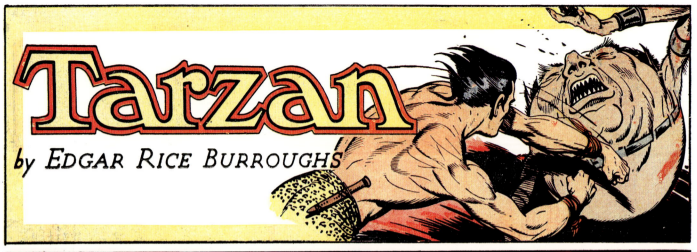

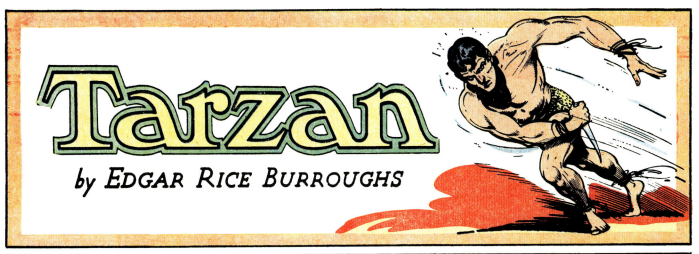

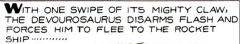

Flash Gordon

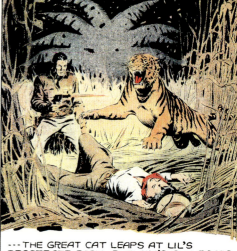

JUNGLE JIM
BY ALEX RAYMOND

With a mixed company of crack Indian and Chinese guerrillas, Jim is off on his dangerous mission---

By dawn, Jim and his men have filtered through the enemy lines and taken cover in a clump of trees. While the men rest, sharp-eyed sentries guard against discovery by the enemy---

Jim summons his lieutenants, Sing Lee and Beardsley: "This ammunition dump is our first objective. We will approach it from three sides and attack at midnight. When our work is done, we will scatter and meet at the ruined temple at midnight tomorrow!"

By dusk, each man is thoroughly familiar with his assignment. At timed intervals throughout the evening, each squad is led into position---

Exactly at midnight, a panther's scream issues from Jim's throat---his men rise like wraiths from the tall, jungle grass and move silently to the attack!

(CONTINUED.)

Flash Gordon

1. Brazor and his men soon overcome Lieutenant Caran's brave resistance and, rushing to the edge of the terrace, see Flash and his friends escaping. They open fire, starting a landslide which sweeps the fugitives from the sheer cliff-face!

2. Dale swings inward to a ledge, dragging Zarkov with her---the fall knocks her out---Zarkov dazedly braces himself as the bodies of Flash and Desira hurtle by---

3. Flash grabs a projecting rock, tearing his hands and almost pulling his mighty arms from their sockets---

4. Both Dale and Zarkov should certainly have been jerked from their ledge, had Flash lost his grip---but he didn't---and Zarkov was able to sustain the shock of Desira's light body. Flash swings himself astride the projection and hauls Desira to safety.

NEXT WEEK: UNDER FIRE

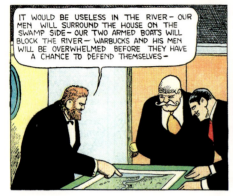

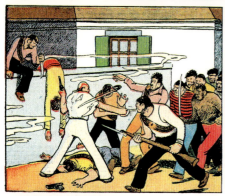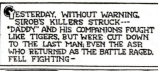

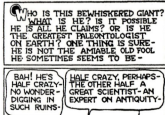

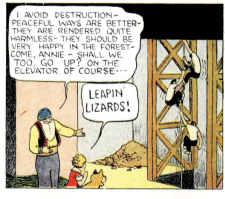

Maw Green

DICK TRACY — 1937 — CHESTER GOULD

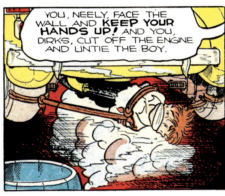

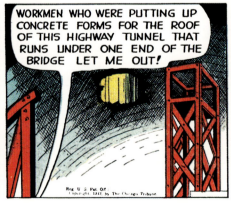

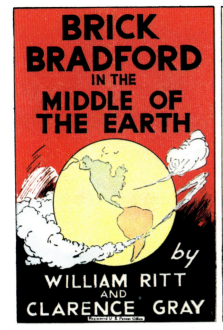

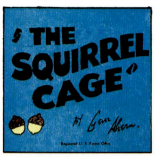

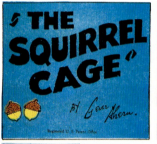
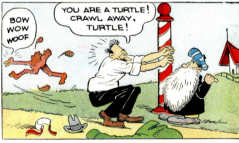
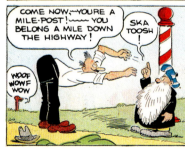

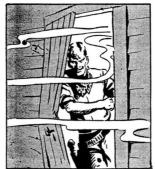

BARNEY BAXTER   1937   FRANK MILLER

JIM HARDY   1937   DICK MOORES

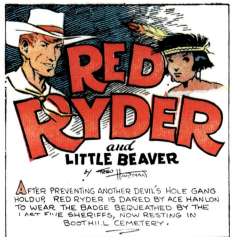

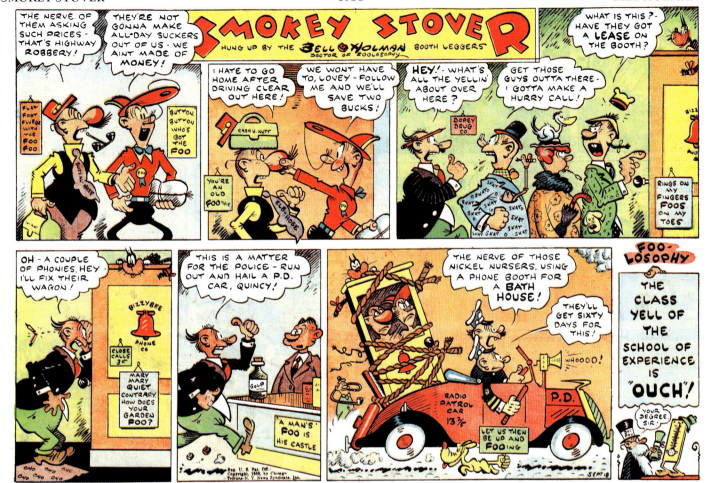
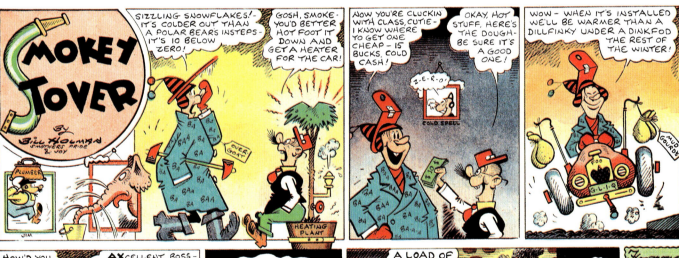

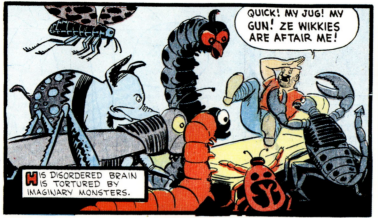

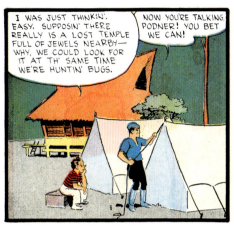

CAPTAIN EASY BY ROY CRANE

CAPTAIN EASY by ROY CRANE

CAPTAIN EASY by ROY CRANE

CAPTAIN EASY BY ROY CRANE

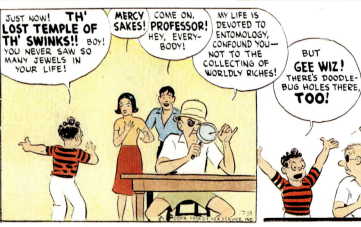

CAPTAIN EASY by ROY CRANE

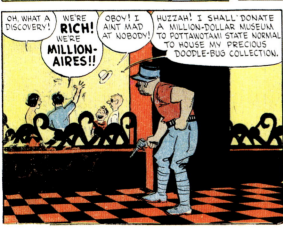

CAPTAIN EASY BY ROY CRANE

CAPTAIN EASY by ROY CRANE

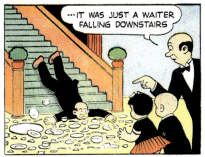

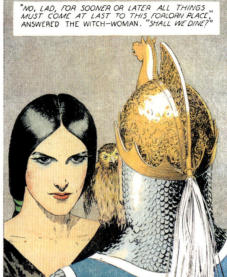

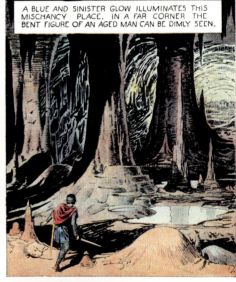

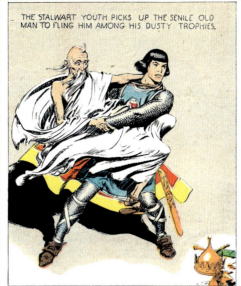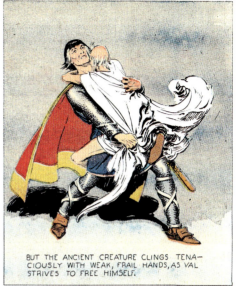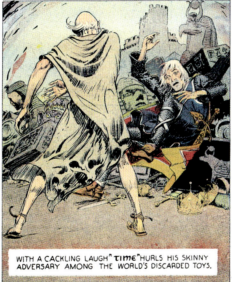

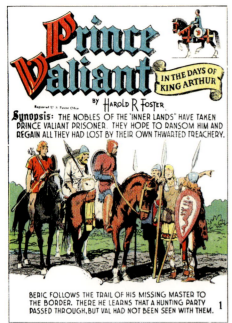

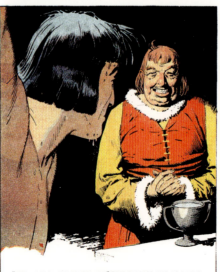

1940–1995

| MYRA NORTH | 1940 | RAY THOMPSON • CHARLES COLL |

| HUCKLEBERRY FINN | 1941 | CLARE VICTOR DWIGGINS |

THE RED KNIGHT   1943   JOHN J. WELCH • JACK W. McGUIRE

BUNKY — 1942 — BILLY DE BECK

  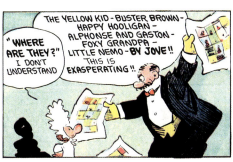

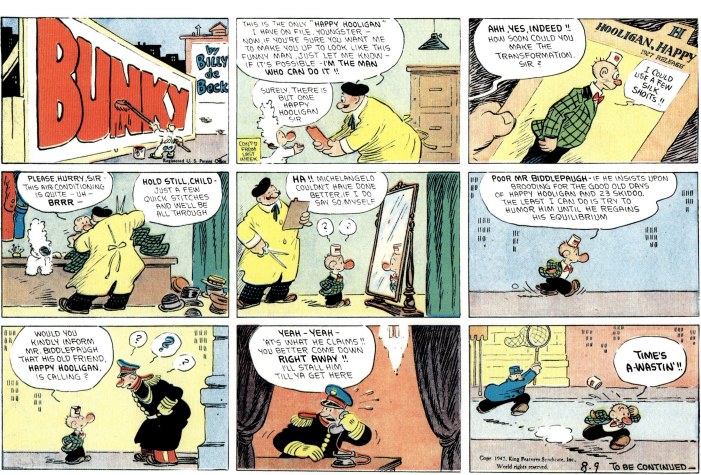

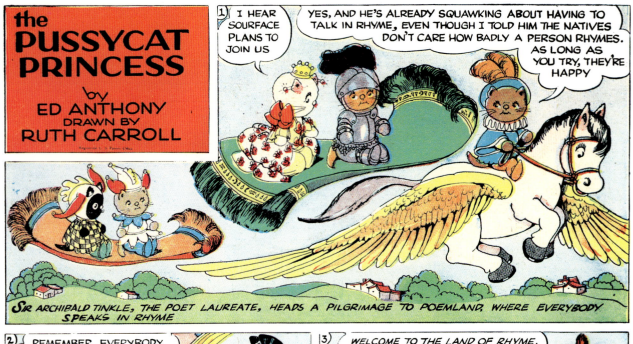

SKIPPY 1942 PERCY CROSBY

SUPERWOMAN 1943 REA IRVIN

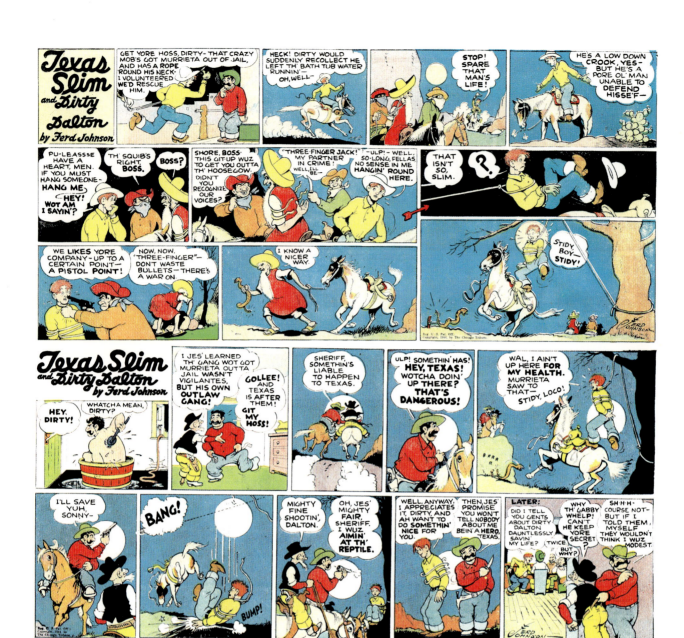

BARNABY 1944 CROCKETT JOHNSON

BATMAN AND ROBIN 1944 BOB KANE

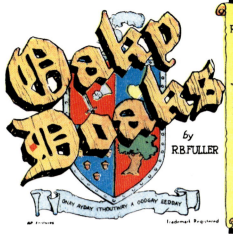

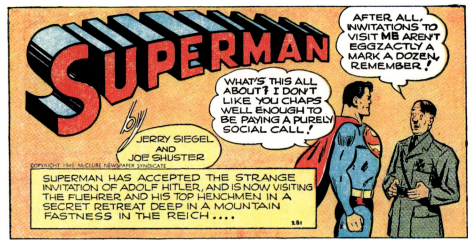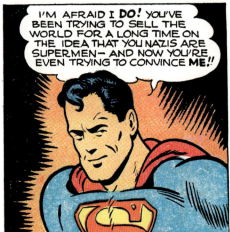

BUZ SAWYER   1947   **ROY CRANE**

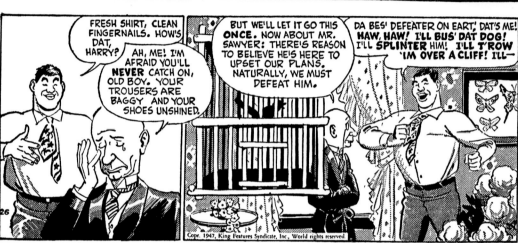

THE SPIRIT 1947 WILL EISNER

The Big New Spirit Book

The Sunday Bulletin

SUNDAY, JULY 20, 1947

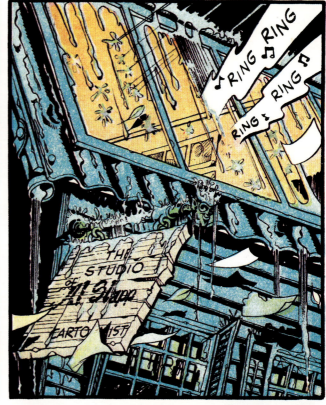

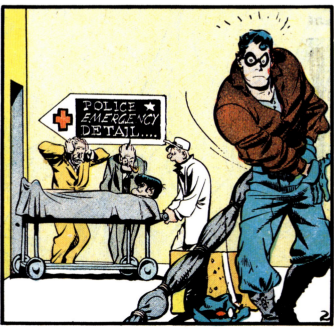

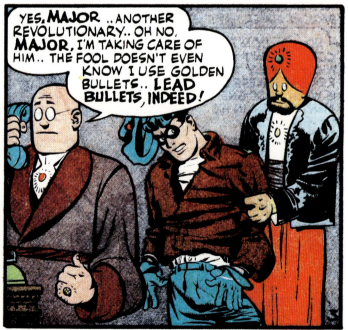

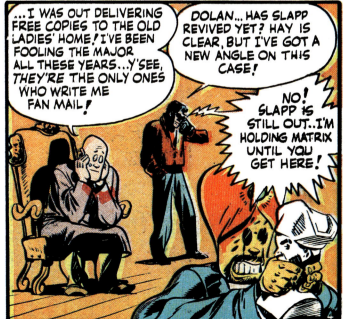

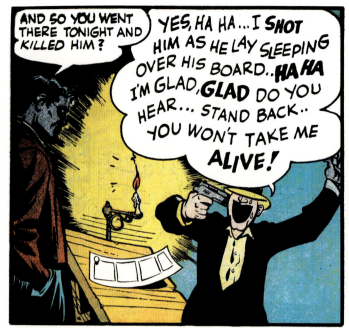

SILVER LININGS 1948 HARVEY KURTZMAN

SAD SACK 1949 GEORGE BAKER

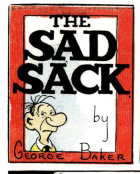

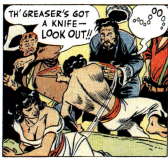

STEVE CANYON 1951 MILTON CANIFF

1954

1957

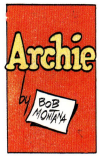

1959

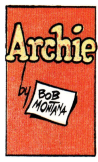

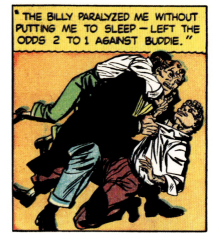

BEETLE BAILEY — 1955 — MORT WALKER

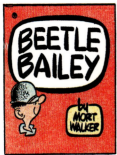

1956

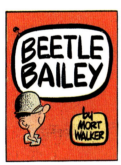

Beetle Bailey 1954 Mort Walker

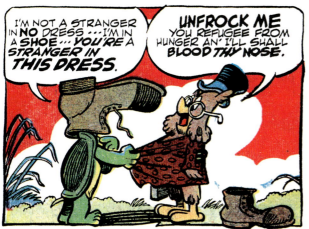

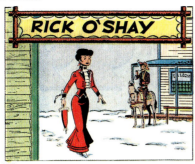

ON STAGE 1960 LEONARD STARR

HI AND LOIS 1962 MORT WALKER • DIK BROWNE

PEANUTS 1964 CHARLES SCHULTZ

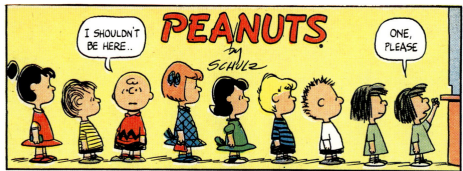

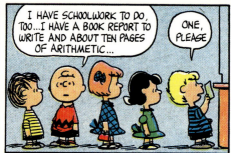

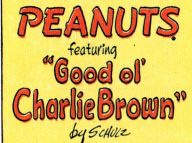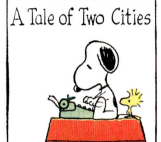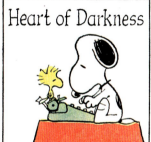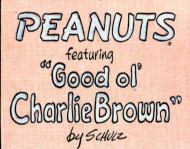

DENNIS THE MENACE — 1966 — HANK KETCHAM

JOHNNY HAZARD — 1967 — FRANK ROBBINS

B.C.   1963   JOHNNY HART

WIZARD OF ID   1969   BRANT PARKER • JOHNNY HART

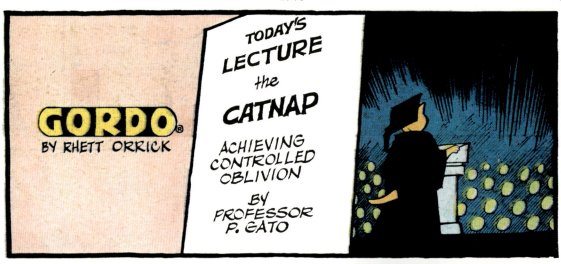

THE FAMILY CIRCUS — 1980 — BIL KEANE

BLOOM COUNTY — 1989 — BERKE BREATHED

MOMMA — 1992 — MEL LAZARUS

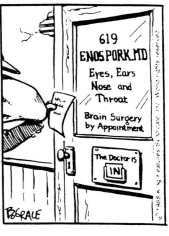

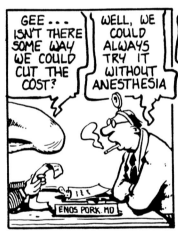

DOONESBURY　　　　　　　　　　1993　　　　　　　　　　G. B. TRUDEAU

FOR BETTER OR WORSE — 1992 — LYNN JOHNSTON

FRANK AND ERNEST — 1993 — BOB THAVES

ZIGGY — 1993 — TOM WILSON

MOTHER GOOSE & GRIMM — 1993 — MIKE PETERS

CATHY — 1994 — CATHY GUISEWITE

ZIPPY THE PINHEAD — 1994 — BILL GRIFFITH

TUMBLEWEEDS — 1994 — T. K. RYAN

SHOE 1993 JEFF MACNELLY

GARFIELD 1994 JIM DAVIS

HAGAR 1994 DIK BROWNE

THE FAR SIDE · 1994 · GARY LARSON

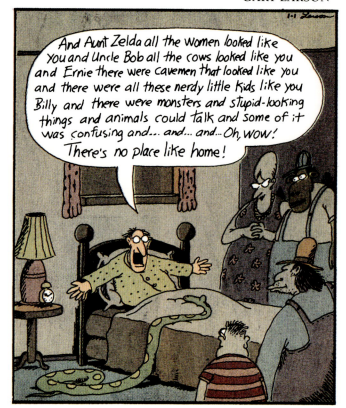

GASOLINE ALLEY · 1991 · JIM SCANCARELLI

TITLE INDEX

Abbie an' Slats, 415
Abie the Agent, 404–405
Adventures of Patsy, The, 278
Adventures of Mr. George, The, 80
Alley Oop, 344–347
Alphonse and Gaston, 48, 51, 52–57, 58–59, 60–61
Archie, 448–449
B.C., 465
Barnaby, 428
Barney Baxter, 382
Barney Google, 129–146, 149
Baron Bean, 107
Batman and Robin, 428
Beetle Bailey, 451–454
Beyond Mars, 447
Billy Bounce, 72
Blondie, 250–273
Bloom County, 467
Bobby Make-Believe, 106
Boob McNutt, 151, 213–215
Brenda Starr, 416
Brick Bradford, 379
Bringing Up Father, 115–117, 147
Bronc Peeler, 240
Brownies in the Philippines, The, 57
Buck Rogers, 226–227
Bungle Family, The, 315–330
Bunky, 419–421
Buster Brown, 96
Buz Sawyer, 432–435
Calvin and Hobbes, 475
Captain and the Kids, The, 39–43, 50, 60–61, 154, 168–171
Captain Easy, 387–403
Casey Ruggles, 445
Cathy, 469
City Shadows, 233–234
Connie, 386
Count Screwloose of Tooloose, 209
Dan Dunn, 237–239
Dave's Delicatessen, 210
Dennis the Menace, 464
Desperate Desmond, 91
Dick Tracy, 375–378
Dingbat Family, The, 91
Donnie, 283
Doonesbury, 473
Dream of the Rarebit Fiend, 67
Embarrassing Moments, 205
Ernie, 470–473
Everett True, 95
Explorigator, The, 77
Family Circus, The, 467
Family Upstairs, The, 84–90
Far Side, The, 476
Felix, 216
Fineheimer Twins, The, 80
Flash Gordon, 362–365
Flyin' Jenny, 425
For Better or Worse, 468
Frank and Ernest, 468
Fritzi Ritz, 406
Garfield, 474
Gasoline Alley, 174–176, 476
Gordo, 466

Gumps, The, 112, 122–128
Hagar, 474
Hairbreadth Harry, 165–166
Hans und Fritz, 39–43, 50, 60–61, 154, 168–171
Happy Hooligan, 49, 60–61, 62–63, 152
Hejji, 284–295
Henry, 299
Hi and Lois, 460
Hogan's Alley, 35–38
Huckleberry Finn, 417–418
Hugo Hercules, 46
Hungry Henrietta, 67
Jerry on the Job, 118–119
Jim Hardy, 382
Jimmy, 66
Joe Palooka, 222–225
Johnny Hazard, 464
Jungle Jim, 362–365
Just Boy, 120
Just Kids, 235
Katzenjammer Kids, The, 39–43, 50, 60–61, 154, 168–171
Kewpies, The, 282
Kin-der-kids, The, 74
Krazy Kat, 98–105
Li'l Abner, 348–353
Little Bears, The, 44
Little Jimmy, 148
Little Joe, 296–297
Little Journeys of Nip and Tuck, The, 79
Little King, The, 274
Little Nemo in Slumberland, 68–71
Little Orphan Annie, 242, 366–374
Little Possum Gang, The, 83
Little Sammy Sneeze, 66
Lulu and Leander, 48
Mamma's Angel Child, 111
Mandrake the Magician, 408
Maud, 64
Mickey Mouse, 228–231
Mike Hammer, 450
Ming Foo, 384
Minute Movies, 330–343
Miss Fury, 424
Momma, 467
Moon Mullins, 185–200
Mother Goose & Grimm, 469
Mr. Skygack, from Mars, 78
Mr. Twee Deedle, 94
Mt. Ararat, 45, 47, 50
Mutt and Jeff, 108–109
Myra North, 417
Nancy, 407
Napoleon, 409
Nebbs, The, 184
Nibsy the Newsboy, 76
Nize Baby, 183
Now Listen Mabel, 110
Oaky Doaks, 429
Old Doc Yak, 93
Old Opie Dilldock's Stories, 81
On Stage, 460
Our Boarding House, 279
Out Our Way, 278
Panhandle Pete, 2

Pa's Imported Son-In-Law, 97
Peanuts, 462–463
Phantom, The, 381–382
Pogo, 455–458
Polly and Her Pals, 155–164
Prince Valiant, 410–412
Pussycat Princess, The, 422
Queer Visitors from the Land of Oz, The, 65
Red Barry, 300–315
Red Knight, The, 418
Red Ryder, 383
Rick O'Shay, 459
Rip Kirby, 431–432
Sad Sack, 444
Salesman Sam, 167
School Days, 206–208
Scorchy Smith, 279–281
Secret Agent X-9, 275–277
Sherlocko the Monk, 92
Shoe, 474
Silk Hat Harry's Divorce Suit, 91
Silver Linings, 443–444
Sir Bagby, 461
Skippy, 182, 423
Slim Jim, 82
Smilin' Jack, 297–298
Smokey Stover, 385
Somebody's Stenog, 180–181
Spirit, The 436–442
Squirrel Cage, The, 380
Steve Canyon, 446
Stumble Inn, 121
Superman, 430
Superwoman, 423
Tailspin Tommy, 232
Tarzan, 355–361
Terry and the Pirates, 245–249
Texas Slim, 426–428
Thimble Theatre, 200–205, 217–221
Thrilling Adventures of Count Bric A Brac, 179
Tillie the Toiler, 150
Tim Tyler's Luck, 236
Tiny Tim, 354
Toonerville Folks, 172–173
Toots and Casper, 153
Tumbleweeds, 469
Upside Downs, The, 73
Us Boys, 91
Wee Willie Winkie's World, 75
Winnie Winkle, 177–178
Wizard of Id, 465
Woozlebeasts, The, 73
Yellow Kid, The, 35–38
Ziggy, 468
Zippy the Pinhead, 469

NAME INDEX

Ahern, Gene, 279, 380
Anderson, Carl, 299
Anthony, Ed, 422
Arriola, Gus, 466
Baker, George, 444
Baum, L. Frank, 65
Bemelmans, Ludwig, 179
Branner, Martin, 177
Breathed, Berke, 467
Browne, Dik, 460, 474
Bushmiller, Ernie, 406, 407
Calkins, Dick, 226
Caniff, Milton, 245–249, 446
Capp, Al, 348–353
Carey, Ed, 97
Carroll, Ruth, 422
Carter, Ad, 235
Chaffin, Glenn, 232
Coll, Charles, 417
Condo, A. D., 78, 95
Cox, Palmer, 57
Crane, Roy, 387–403, 432–435
Crosby, Percy, 182, 233, 423
Dart, Harry Grant, 77
Davis, Jim, 474
Davis, Phil, 408
De Beck, Billy, 129–146, 149, 419–421
Dirks, Rudolph, 39–43, 50, 60–61
Disney, Walt, 228
Dorgan, "Tad", 91
Dwiggins, Clare Victor, 206, 417–418
Eisner, Will, 436–442
Elias, Lee, 447
Ewer, Raymond Crawford, 82
Falk, Lee, 381–382, 408
Feininger, Lyonel, 74, 75
Fera, A. C., 120
Fisher, Bud, 108–109
Fisher, Ham, 222
Forrest, Hal, 232
Foster, Hal, 355, 410–412
Fox, Fontaine, 172
Fuller, R. B., 429
Godwin, Frank, 386
Goldberg, Rube, 151, 213
Gould, Chester, 375–378
Gould, Will, 300–315
Grace, Bud, 468–471
Graff, Mel, 278
Gray, Clarence, 379
Gray, Harold, 242, 366–374
Griffith, Bill, 473
Gross, Milt, 183, 209, 210
Gruelle, John, 94
Guisewite, Cathy, 473
Hackney, B., 461
Hackney, R., 461
Hamlin, V. T., 344–347
Hammett, Dashiell, 275–277
Harman, Fred, 240, 383
Hart, Johnny, 465
Hayward, A. E., 180
Herriman, George, 84–90, 91, 98–105, 107, 110, 121, 205
Hershfield, Harry, 91, 404–405
Hess, Sol, 184

Hoban, Walter C., 118–119
Hogarth, Burne, 356–361
Holman, Bill, 385
Howarth, Frank M., 48
Irvin, Rea, 423
Johnson, Crockett, 428
Johnson, Ferd, 426–428
Johnston, Lynn, 472
Kahles, C. W., 165–166
Kahles, Charles, 72
Kane, Bob, 428
Keane, Bil, 467
Keaton, Russell, 425
Kelly, Walt, 455–458
Ketcham, Hank, 464
King, Frank, 106 174
Knerr, Harold, 80, 154, 168–171
Koerner, J., 45
Kurtzman, Harvey, 443–444
Larson, Gary, 476
Lazarus, Mell, 467
Leffingwell, Ed, 296–297
Link, Stanley, 354
Lynde, Stan, 459
MacNelly, Jeff, 474
Mager, Gus, 92
Marsh, Norman, 237–239
Martin, H. B., 49
McBride, Clifford, 409
McCay, Winsor, 66, 67, 68–71
McClure, Darrell, 283
McDougall, Walt, 65
McGuire, Jack W., 418
McManus, George, 2, 76, 115–117, 147
McNamara, Tom, 91
Messick, Dale, 416
Miller, Frank, 382
Mills, Tarpe, 424
Montana, Bob, 448–449
Moore, Ray, 381–382
Moores, Dick, 382
Mosley, Zack, 297–298
Murphy, Jimmy, 153
Neill, John R., 79
Nowlan, Phil, 226
O'Neill, Rose, 282
Opper, Frederick, 48, 49, 51, 52–57, 58–59, 60–61, 62–63, 64, 152
Outcault, R. F., 35–38, 96
Parker, Brant, 465
Payne, C. M., 83
Peters, Mike, 473
Raymond, Alex, 275–277, 362–365, 431–432
Ritt, William, 379
Robbins, Ed, 450
Robbins, Frank, 464
Ross, Penny, 111
Ryan, T. K., 473
Scancarelli, Jim, 476
Schulz, Charles, 462–463
Segar, E. C., 200, 217
Seuss, Dr., 284–295
Shuster, Joe, 430
Sickles, Noel, 279–281
Siegel, Jerry, 430
Smith, Sidney, 93, 112, 122–128

Soglow, Otto, 274
Spillane, Mickey, 450
Starr, Leonard, 460
Sterrett, Cliff, 155–164
Sullivan, Pat, 216
Swan, George, 167
Swinnerton, James, 44, 46, 47, 50, 66, 148
Thaves, Bob, 472
Thompson, Ray, 417
Trudeau, G. B., 471
Tufts, Warren, 445
Tuthill, Harry J., 315–330
Van Buren, Raeburn, 415
Verbeck, Gustave, 73
Walker, Mort, 451–454, 460
Walsh, Brandon, 384
Watterson, Bill, 475
Wead, Frank, 425
Welch, John J., 418
Wells, M. L., 81
Westover, Russ, 150
Wheelan, Ed, 330–343
Willard, Fred, 185
Williams, J. R., 278
Williamson, Jack, 447
Wilson, Tom, 472
Young, Chic, 250–273
Young, Lyman, 236

COPYRIGHT CREDITS

Every comic strip episode reprinted in these pages carries its own individual copyright notice for the date of original publication, with the applicable year and title repeated at the top of the page on which the episodes appear. For convenience of reference, this data is grouped here as well. The following titles have been organized under their appropriate copyright owners, and all those listed are currently in copyright, with all rights reserved, as designated here. In general all strips with a publication date later than 1920 are in copyright control and cannot be reprinted or excerpted in any way without specific permission from the copyright and/or trademark owner.

In a number of cases, the strips listed below are copyrighted by their artists and authors, who have elected to distribute their work through a syndicate operation. Where this separate copyright ownership specification has been requested, we have assigned such individual copyright listings under the distributing syndicate's name, title by title.

KING FEATURES SYNDICATE is the copyright owner of: *Skippy, The Katzenjammer Kids, Bringing Up Father, Barney Google, Bunky, Prince Valiant, Flash Gordon, Little Jimmy, Tillie the Toiler, Boob McNutt, Happy Hooligan, Toots and Casper, Just Boy (Elmer), Krazy Kat, Stumble Inn, Polly and Her Pals, Felix the Cat, Jerry on the Job, Beetle Bailey, Rip Kirby, Buz Sawyer, Steve Canyon, Hi and Lois, Archie, Hejji, Squirrel Cage, Mandrake the Magician, Brick Bradford, Blondie, Just Kids, The Pussycat Princess, Henry, The Little King,* the *Percey Crosby American Weekly* covers, *Tim Tyler's Luck, Donnie, Red Barry, Ming Foo, Secret Agent X-9, The Kewpies, Thimble Theatre (Popeye), The Phantom, Ernie, Family Circus, Barney Baxter, Dave's Delicatessen, Johnny Hazard, Hagar the Horrible.* All reprinted by special permission.

TRIBUNE MEDIA SERVICES: *Gasoline Alley, Smokey Stover, Smilin' Jack, Dick Tracy, Moon Mullins, Shoe, Mother Goose and Grimm, Little Orphan Annie, On Stage, Beyond Mars, Little Joe, Texas Slim and Dirty Dalton, Terry and the Pirates, Rick O'Shay, Brenda Starr, Tiny Tim, Winnie Winkle.* All reprinted by permission.

UNITED MEDIA*: *Gordo, Nancy, Casey Ruggles, Peanuts, Wash Tubbs, Captain Easy, Alley Oop, Myra North, Frank and Ernest, Our Boarding House, Out Our Way, Fritzi Ritz, Red Ryder, Garfield, Jim Hardy.*

*NEA and United Features, as credited on many of the above listed strips as reprinted in these pages.

UNIVERSAL PRESS SYNDICATE is the distributor and permissions agency for the following independently copyrighted titles: *Calvin and Hobbes,* copyright Bill Watterson; *Cathy,* copyright Cathy Guisewite; *Doonesbury,* copyright G. B. Trudeau; *The Far Side,* copyright Farworks, Inc.; *Ziggy,* copyright Ziggy & Friends, Inc. All rights reserved by the individually designated copyright holders for each listed title.

CREATORS SYNDICATE: *B. C., Wizard of Id, Momma.*

WILL EISNER STUDIOS, INC.: *The Spirit* is a trademark of Will Eisner Studios, Inc. © 1947.

CAPP ENTERPRISES, INC.: *Li'l Abner, Abbie and Slats.* All rights reserved.

DC COMICS: *Superman* is a trademark of DC Comics © 1945. Used with permission. All rights reserved. *Batman* and all related elements are trademark and copyright © 1944 DC Comics. Used with permission. All rights reserved.

NORTH AMERICAN SYNDICATE: *Dennis the Menace, Tumbleweeds.*

WASHINGTON POST WRITERS GROUP: *Bloom County.*

THE WALT DISNEY COMPANY: *Mickey Mouse, Silly Symphonies.*

OKEEFENOKEE GLEE AND PERLOO, INC: *Pogo.*

GEORGE BAKER/ BELL SYNDICATE: *The Sad Sack.*

MICKEY SPILLANE: *Mike Hammer.*

ERB, INC.: *Tarzan.* All rights reserved.

Every reasonable effort has been made to locate the present copyright holders of certain properties once distributed by now defunct syndicates or other parties. Any information regarding such copyright holders would be appreciated by the publisher.

In addition to the books collecting various contemporary comic strips available at most bookstores, the following publishers specialize in collections of many classic comic strips which are available at comic book shops or by requesting a free catalog from each in writing or by using their toll-free number.

Kitchen Sink Press, Inc.
320 Riverside Drive, Northampton, MA 01060.
1 800 365-7465

Fantagraphics Books
7563 Lake City Way NE, Seattle, WA 98115.
1 800 657-1100

NBM
185 Madison Avenue, Ste. 1504, New York, NY 10016.
1 800 886-1223

BILL BLACKBEARD learned to read from the newspaper comics long before he started to kindergarten in Lawrence, Indiana, where he was born in 1926. Preferring to read what interested him thereafter, he put in desk time in school and college, sometimes baffling his English and history professors with esoteric and detailed references to centuries-old writers and events they had never heard of as a lark to relieve classroom boredom. Selling his first story to *Weird Tales* in 1944, he served in the U.S. Army's 89th Cavalry Squadron in France and Germany in combat and occupation duty, carrying a first edition of Dickens' *Martin Chuzzlewit*—"the funniest novel in the English language" as he terms it—in his knapsack through all engagements as relief reading. After years as a writer and active science fiction fan (and comic strip researcher) he founded the San Francisco Academy of Comic Art in 1967, the only non-profit research center devoted to the cross-reference study of all the narrative arts in accessible, side-by-side collections, from ballads, drama, genre fiction in all divisions, film, popular periodical fiction, children's fiction, newspaper comic strips, graphic novels, dime novels, comic books, story papers, penny dreadfuls, etc., etc., from the 1500s to date. He has edited or written over two hundred books to date, primarily in his chosen area of particular expertise, the comic strip.

DALE CRAIN has served as designer and art director for a diverse array of prestigious publishers including Penguin Books, Doubleday, Hearst, Chilton, RAW Books, Fantagraphics Books, Kitchen Sink Press and *The New York Times*. He is the recipient of two *Print* Magazine awards for design, and three Harvey Awards for art direction. A specialist in the field of comics and cartooning, he has designed and packaged volumes reprinting the work of such distinguished artists as Robert Crumb, Jules Feiffer, Winsor McCay, Milton Caniff, George Herriman, Lyonel Feininger and Ralph Steadman. In addition to his work on such archival productions, he has also lent his talents to virtually every comic book publisher in the United States.

JAMES VANCE is a writer, editor and journalist who has worked in the fine and popular arts since the late 1970s. His play *Stations* was selected to represent the United States in the 1981 World Theater Festival in Monte Carlo, and his television documentary "Climbing Jacob's Ladder" won the National Conference of Christians and Jews' 1993 Media Award. His first work in the comics field, the graphic novel *Kings in Disguise,* received Harvey and Eisner Awards in 1989. He has subsequently written scripts for Kitchen Sink Press, DC Comics, Dark Horse Comics and Big Entertainment. As editor-in-chief for Kitchen Sink, he supervised books collecting the work of Al Capp, V. T. Hamlin, Will Eisner, Harvey Kurtzman and other legendary cartoonists.